# Foreword

## In a World Full of Confusion: How Can \

In today's world, we face confusion, brokenness, and a constant search for meaning. How can we find joy and truly connect with God? These aren't just abstract questions—they impact our everyday lives.

I graduated from Calvin Seminary in 1987, trained in theological studies. Many people would call this the study of Christian religion. During my education, I was also taught to respect the social sciences—fields like psychology and sociology—especially when it came to mental health, education, relationships, and human development. These sciences provided helpful theories for behavior, therapy, and human well-being. Yet, even as I studied these fields, I couldn't help but notice that many of the "new" ideas in psychology were already present in the Bible, ideas that had been there all along.

When we founded the **Christian Leaders Institute** in 2006, we began with traditional seminary subjects like biblical and theological studies. Our initial goal was to offer free online ministry training to anyone who felt called to serve. But by 2013, something deeper began to emerge. We realized that the Bible doesn't just address eternal life; it speaks powerfully to the human condition now. It provides a hope that isn't just distant but real—hope through the God who created us and redeemed us. The Bible became our guide for understanding humanity. By 2014, we launched the **Christian Leaders Alliance** to credential ministers—volunteer and career ministers—who could share this hope.

But as we moved forward, a deeper question surfaced: Why had the church handed over so much ground to the social sciences when the Bible already offered guidance for flourishing in life? Why had modern social sciences shifted to a place where God was not only ignored but considered irrelevant?

## The Early Church: A Model for Social Services with God

The early Christian church had a different way of doing things. The first leaders were trained and recognized as ministers not just to offer spiritual guidance but to provide practical, everyday help. They offered something the world hadn't seen before—care that included God in the process. And it wasn't just about eternal hope; it was about thriving in this life.

But over time, the church shifted its focus, centering more on theological studies and the soul's relationship with God. This change left a gap in how the church addressed the practical aspects of human flourishing. Social sciences—modern psychology, sociology, and therapy—stepped in, often leaving God out entirely. Christianity was reduced to "spiritual things," while the practical side of life was handed over to secular experts.

## Reclaiming the Role of God in Human Flourishing

Christianity shouldn't only be about eternal hope—it must also focus on how we live now. It's time for Christianity to reclaim its place in the study of human well-being. Instead of calling it

"Christian social sciences," we call it **Ministry Sciences**—a study of the human experience that includes God.

Here's the conflict: Modern social sciences, especially in their postmodern and metamodern forms, have largely excluded God. They analyze life through a lens that ignores or denies the divine, leaving us with fragmented answers. Postmodernism aggressively shut God out, claiming that truth is subjective, and nothing is real. Metamodernism swings between optimism and doubt, attempting to merge modern confidence with postmodern skepticism—but still leaves out God.

This worldview creates confusion. A society without God drifts, searching for meaning but never finding a solid foundation. How do we explain life's ups and downs? How do we face our personal failures? The modern world offers little comfort beyond "self-help" techniques that feel shallow in the face of real brokenness.

**Ministry Sciences: Inviting God Back into the Picture**

We reject the approaches that shut God out. We want to invite God into every part of our lives. We know we're broken—"for all have sinned and fall short of the glory of God" (Romans 3:23, WEB). But we're also redeemed through Christ, renewed by the Holy Spirit. Life is tough, and we need God in our minds, hearts, and communities. **Ministry Sciences** is about helping others live in this truth, experiencing transformation that comes from being shaped into the image of God (Romans 12:2).

The early church spread not just because of its theology but because of its care for people—volunteer ministers, part-time servants, and career ministers offered services freely, helping others thrive. Ministry Sciences aims to return to this model, offering free training and credentialing without making ministers dependent on a paycheck.

**A New Path for Those Who Want to Make a Difference**

This book isn't about fighting with those who exclude God. They've made their choice. Nor is it about judging those who follow modern, postmodern, or metamodern ideas. Instead, it's an invitation to explore a new path—one that brings transformation by embracing the reality of God in our lives and ministries.

**Who Should Read This Book?**

- **Christians:** Deepen your faith by seeing how God is active in all parts of life.
- **Officiants, Ministers, Coaches, and Chaplains:** Gain practical tools and insights for leading others.
- **Christian Counselors and Therapists:** Learn how to integrate faith into your practice for holistic healing.
- **The Curious:** Explore how including God changes everything about how we see ourselves and the world.

Imagine a world where anyone can access free ministry training, where grassroots credentialing allows leaders from all backgrounds to serve. Imagine church leaders studying **Ministry Sciences**, gaining new skills to minister to their communities, and spreading hope. This is the goal: to empower a new generation of ministers who will offer real hope in a broken world.

We invite you to explore **Ministry Sciences**, where God is not only acknowledged but celebrated. If you want God to shape your life and ministry, join us on this journey. You'll discover a new way of living that's rooted in truth and filled with the transforming power of God's love. Together, we can bring His hope to a world that desperately needs it.

# The Study of the Means of Grace

### The Means of Divine Transformation in Ministry: A Sample of God's Grace at Work

In today's world, many turn to social sciences like psychology, sociology, and counseling to address their challenges and needs. While these sciences offer helpful insights into human behavior, they often exclude God from the process of transformation. Practitioners trained in these fields are generally taught to separate religious beliefs from their methods, meaning they may not acknowledge how God can work in someone's life to bring healing and change.

But in the realm of ministry, the story is different. **Divine means**, or **means of grace**, are channels through which God's power, love, and transformation flow into the lives of believers. These are not just ordinary practices or techniques—they are ways God interacts with and blesses His people. While the social sciences may hit a ceiling in what they can offer, **divine means connect us directly to Heaven's healing**, which is available for everyone who believes.

What follows is a sample of these powerful means of grace, highlighting how God's presence can transform lives in ways that the social sciences, limited by excluding God, cannot achieve.

## Prayer: A Direct Line to Heaven

While counseling sessions or group therapy may be helpful, they cannot replace the unique power of **prayer**. Prayer is a means of grace that invites God directly into our situations, whether it's to express worship, confess sins, or ask for His help. The Bible shows us the vastness of prayer's potential:

- **Adoration**: Praising God for who He is.
    - *"I will exalt you, my God, the King. I will praise your name forever and ever."* (Psalm 145:1-3, WEB)
- **Confession**: Seeking forgiveness and renewal.
    - *"If we confess our sins, he is faithful and righteous to forgive us the sins, and to cleanse us from all unrighteousness."* (1 John 1:9, WEB)

- **Healing**: Bringing emotional, physical, and spiritual healing.
    - *"The prayer of faith will heal him who is sick, and the Lord will raise him up."* (James 5:15, WEB)

Social sciences can't provide the spiritual breakthrough that comes when someone experiences the **power of God through prayer**. Therapy may analyze your problems, but prayer delivers solutions directly from Heaven.

## The Word of God: Living and Active

The Bible is not just a religious text—it is **alive and active**, a tool for spiritual growth and transformation. In Ministry Sciences, the **Word of God** is central because it is through Scripture that God speaks to us, guiding and correcting us in ways no human wisdom can match.

- *"For the word of God is living and active, sharper than any two-edged sword."* (Hebrews 4:12, WEB)

While social sciences might use human understanding to solve problems, the **Bible is divinely inspired** and offers a supernatural insight that far exceeds what human knowledge can provide. It's not just about learning; it's about being transformed by God's truth.

## Personal Devotion: Living Out the Seven Connections

Daily prayer, Bible reading, and reflecting on God's Word are essential to a Christian's spiritual growth. These personal devotions are reproducible habits that allow believers to stay connected with God, ensuring their lives are continually shaped by His presence. These practices provide guidance, hope, and strength.

- *"Your word is a lamp to my feet, and a light for my path."* (Psalm 119:105, WEB)

In contrast, social sciences can help with emotional self-regulation, but they often miss the deeper transformation that comes from **walking daily with God**. Therapy might help manage symptoms, but devotion to God offers **wholeness**.

## The Transformative Power of Connection with God

While therapy helps people understand themselves, **a relationship with Christ** leads to true transformation. It changes one's identity, bringing them from darkness into light, from guilt into grace, from brokenness into wholeness.

- *"Therefore if anyone is in Christ, he is a new creation."* (2 Corinthians 5:17, WEB)

Social sciences, with their human-centered focus, cannot offer this kind of deep **spiritual rebirth**. Only through Christ's atoning work can someone truly experience new life.

## The Work of the Holy Spirit: More Than Human Effort

The Holy Spirit plays an essential role in empowering and equipping believers for ministry. Where social sciences rely solely on human effort, the Holy Spirit brings supernatural power, gifting, and guidance.

- *"But you will receive power when the Holy Spirit has come upon you."* (Acts 1:8, WEB)

The Holy Spirit provides gifts like wisdom, knowledge, faith, and healing—tools that equip believers to serve others in ways no psychology or social theory could ever replicate.

## The Fruit of the Spirit: Beyond Self-Improvement

In a world filled with self-help books and therapies aimed at improving oneself, the Bible offers something much more profound—the **Fruit of the Spirit**. These virtues, grown by the Holy Spirit within us, go beyond mere self-improvement and reflect a life fully surrendered to God.

- *"But the fruit of the Spirit is love, joy, peace, patience, kindness, goodness, faith, gentleness, and self-control."* (Galatians 5:22-23, WEB)

While the social sciences may teach mindfulness or coping strategies, the **Holy Spirit grows lasting spiritual fruit** that transforms not only our inner life but also our relationships with others.

## Worship: Experiencing God's Presence

Worship—whether corporate or personal—brings us into the **very presence of God**. In moments of worship, we encounter His power and grace, renewing our spirits and providing strength.

- *"For where two or three are gathered together in my name, there I am in the middle of them."* (Matthew 18:20, WEB)

While music therapy might elevate mood, only **worship** can bring the transforming power of the Holy Spirit into our hearts and minds.

## Sacraments: Baptism and Communion

Sacraments like **baptism** and **communion** are physical testimonies of spiritual realities. Baptism marks new life in Christ, while communion reminds us of His sacrifice and promises.

- *"Go and make disciples of all nations, baptizing them in the name of the Father and of the Son and of the Holy Spirit."* (Matthew 28:19, WEB)

Therapies and rituals in the social sciences might provide closure or connection, but the sacraments do more—they bring God's **grace** into our very being, reminding us of our eternal relationship with Him.

## Fellowship: Building True Christian Community

Fellowship with other believers creates a community that provides support, encouragement, and accountability. It's not just about being around people—it's about growing together in faith and purpose.

- *"They continued steadfastly in the apostles' teaching and fellowship, in the breaking of bread, and prayer."* (Acts 2:42, WEB)

While group therapy offers shared experiences, **Christian fellowship** builds spiritual relationships that help individuals grow in their walk with God, supporting one another toward maturity in Christ.

## Conclusion: Divine Means vs. Social Sciences

In summary, while the social sciences provide valuable insights into human behavior, they are limited by their exclusion of God. They stop short of the kind of **deep, lasting transformation** that comes through divine means.

**Prayer, Scripture, the work of the Holy Spirit, and the sacraments** are just a few examples of how God connects Heaven with Earth, healing our sorrows and making us whole. These means of grace offer a transformation that goes far beyond anything the social sciences can offer. They connect us with God's power, His presence, and His purpose for our lives.

So, as we continue in ministry, we must not overlook or underestimate these divine means. They are not just rituals or good habits—they are the very lifeblood of transformation in the Christian journey. And through them, **God's healing and redemption are made real in our lives**.

## Further Reading List on Divine Transformation in Ministry

1. **"Prayer: Experiencing Awe and Intimacy with God" by Timothy Keller**

    - Keller delves into the purpose and power of prayer, exploring how it serves as a channel to connect with God. This book is a deep dive into the theological foundations of prayer and its transformative effect on the believer's life.

2. **"The Power of a Praying Life" by Stormie Omartian**

    - Omartian's practical approach helps readers understand how prayer can shape their everyday lives and deepen their relationship with God, making prayer an essential means of grace.

3. **"The Spirit of the Disciplines: Understanding How God Changes Lives" by Dallas Willard**

    - Willard explains the spiritual disciplines, including prayer, worship, and Bible reading, as means through which God transforms our lives. This book contrasts divine transformation with secular self-improvement efforts.

4. **"Knowing God" by J.I. Packer**

    - Packer explores the significance of knowing God personally, focusing on how divine knowledge through the Word of God leads to a transformed life. It's an essential read on the impact of Scripture in Christian living.

5. **"Living in the Spirit: Drawing Us into the Life of God" by George T. Montague**

    - This book explores the role of the Holy Spirit in the Christian life, examining how spiritual gifts and the fruit of the Spirit are essential for divine transformation.

6. **"Celebration of Discipline: The Path to Spiritual Growth" by Richard J. Foster**

    - Foster discusses the classic spiritual disciplines—prayer, fasting, study, worship—and how they serve as channels for receiving God's grace and transformation.

7. **"The Power of the Blood of Jesus" by Andrew Murray**

    - Murray explains the significance of Christ's blood in atonement, cleansing, and transformation, emphasizing its foundational role in the Christian life and the means of grace through which we experience redemption.

8. **"Worship Matters: Leading Others to Encounter the Greatness of God" by Bob Kauflin**

    - Kauflin dives into the importance of worship as a means of experiencing God's presence. This book highlights worship's transformative power within corporate and personal settings.

9. **"The Dynamics of Spiritual Gifts" by William McRae**

    - This resource focuses on the gifts of the Spirit and how they empower believers for ministry and service. It examines the role of spiritual gifts in personal and corporate transformation.

10. **"The Great Divorce" by C.S. Lewis**

    - Though not a theological treatise, this allegorical book provides a vivid picture of the transformative power of choice and God's grace, contrasting earthly limitations with divine possibilities.

11. **"The Sacraments: Symbol, Meaning, and Discipleship" by Bernard Cooke**

    - Cooke explores the significance of sacraments like baptism and communion in Christian life, explaining how these acts connect believers with God's grace and bring about transformation.

12. **"The Pursuit of God" by A.W. Tozer**

    - Tozer's classic work challenges readers to seek God passionately. It emphasizes how God meets us through divine means, transforming our lives from the inside out.

13. **"The Discipline of Grace: God's Role and Our Role in the Pursuit of Holiness" by**

**Jerry Bridges**

- o Bridges explains the balance between divine grace and human effort in spiritual growth, providing insights on how grace empowers and transforms believers through spiritual disciplines.

14 **"Holy Spirit: The Missing Person in the Trinity" by R.T. Kendall**

- o This book takes a deep dive into the role of the Holy Spirit, exploring how His work in our lives is a fundamental means of grace that brings about personal transformation and spiritual growth.

15 **"Systematic Theology" by Wayne Grudem**

- o Grudem's comprehensive guide covers key doctrines, including the work of the Holy Spirit, the Word of God, and sacraments, emphasizing their role as means of grace in the transformation of believers.

# What is Ministry Sciences?

## What is Ministry Sciences: A Testimony-Based, Evidence-Confirming Approach to Discernment, Healing, Transformation, and Wholeness

The call to Christian ministry is both challenging and rewarding. This book introduces the idea of **Ministry Sciences**—an organized study of different areas of ministry that blend biblical teaching, theology, philosophy, and practical skills. Ministry Sciences combines deep thinking with real-world actions, recognizing the social issues that impact today's ministry work. It's not just about learning; it's about taking action, built on the unchanging truths of the Bible, to serve effectively in God's kingdom.

Training Christians and ministry leaders through Ministry Sciences is more important now than ever. With the fast changes in today's world, ministries need to be well-rounded, based on solid theology and practical skills. This book provides the tools needed to serve wisely, with integrity and compassion.

At its core, Ministry Sciences is rooted in the Bible. It takes the wisdom from Scripture to guide us in today's world. The Apostle Paul's words to Timothy remind us of the importance of continuous learning: "Be diligent in these things. Give yourself wholly to them, that your progress may be evident to all" (1 Timothy 4:15-16, WEB). This highlights the importance of always growing and improving in ministry, which is a key part of this book.

Paul also talks about equipping believers for ministry in Ephesians 4:11-12: "He gave some to be apostles; and some, prophets; and some, evangelists; and some, pastors and teachers; for the perfecting of the saints, for the work of the ministry." Ministry Sciences takes this calling seriously, preparing leaders who know theology and philosophy and are ready to apply them practically in today's world.

This book is an invitation to dive deep into ministry, combining biblical knowledge with practical tools to serve effectively in diverse settings. Through this exploration, **"Ministry Sciences: A Comprehensive Guide to Modern Ministry Practices"** aims to inspire, challenge, and equip you for your calling in God's kingdom.

As we begin this journey, we remember the words of the Apostle Peter: "As each has received a gift, employ it in serving one another... so that in all things God may be glorified through Jesus Christ" (1 Peter 4:10-11, WEB).

Welcome to the transformative world of Ministry Sciences.

## My Journey to Ministry Sciences – A Testimony

I'm Henry Reyenga, and my journey started at Dordt College, where I earned a degree in Philosophy in 1983. Then, I graduated from Calvin Theological Seminary with a Master of Divinity in 1987 and was ordained in 1988. My wife, Pam, and I planted four churches together, which shaped our calling.

In 2001, we started what would become the Christian Leaders Institute (CLI), officially launching it in 2006. Later, in 2014, the Christian Leaders Alliance was created. CLI has since enrolled hundreds of thousands of students, and the Alliance has ordained over 6,000 ministers. This book is a result of these experiences and is a testimony to God's transformative power at work in ministry.

## What is Ministry Sciences?

Ministry Sciences is the organized study of ministry, combining biblical, theological, and philosophical ideas with the practical side of ministry. This field covers a wide range of topics, including social sciences related to ministry, like coaching, counseling, pastoral care, chaplaincy, communication, teaching, preaching, and leadership.

The goal of Ministry Sciences is not just to give knowledge but to create effective ministers who understand theology and can apply it practically to the real world. This approach aims to equip leaders who walk with God and can meet the challenges of modern-day ministry.

## Why Ministry Sciences Matters

The world is changing fast, and ministry is more complex than ever. From the influence of technology to the impact of postmodern thinking, today's ministers need new skills. Ministry Sciences meets this need by providing education that equips leaders to think critically, act compassionately, and lead effectively in today's world.

Ministry Sciences isn't just for those working in churches. It's a valuable resource for anyone called to lead, whether in their local church or community. Ministry Sciences empowers Christians to serve as volunteer, part-time, or full-time ministers, bringing ministry opportunities to many.

## The Areas Covered by Ministry Sciences

Ministry Sciences includes:

- **Theological Studies**: Understanding the Bible and core Christian beliefs.
- **Philosophical Studies**: Exploring Christian philosophy and how it helps us understand God's design for life.
- **Practical Ministry Skills**: Developing skills in counseling, leadership, pastoral care, and church administration.
- **Innovative Ministry Practices**: Using modern tools like technology to enhance ministry work.
- **Interdisciplinary Integration**: Learning from fields like psychology, sociology, and other social sciences to deepen ministry impact.

Throughout this book, we will explore each of these areas in detail, showing how Ministry Sciences is essential for personal growth and for making a broader impact on the world.

## Further Reading:

- *The Myth of Religious Neutrality* by Roy Clouser
- *A New Critique of Theoretical Thought* by Herman Dooyeweerd
- *The Madness of Crowds* by Douglas Murray
- *Desiring the Kingdom* by James K. A. Smith
- *Christ and Culture* by H. Richard Niebuhr
- *Pastoral Theology: A Global Vision* by Derek Tidball
- *The Pastor: A Memoir* by Eugene H. Peterson
- *Systematic Theology: An Introduction to Biblical Doctrine* by Wayne Grudem
- *The Purpose Driven Church* by Rick Warren
- *The Emotionally Healthy Church* by Peter Scazzero
- *Spiritual Disciplines for the Christian Life* by Donald S. Whitney
- *The Wounded Healer* by Henri J. M. Nouwen
- *Preaching: Communicating Faith in an Age of Skepticism* by Timothy Keller
- *The Confessions* by St. Augustine
- *Knowing God* by J.I. Packer
- *The Divine Conspiracy* by Dallas Willard

# Different Approaches to Thriving

## Study Approaches to Social Thriving: Christian, Modernist, and Postmodern

# Perspectives

# Understanding Religious Ground Motives: Christian, Modernist, and Postmodern Views

## Introduction to Religious Ground Motives

The Dutch philosopher Dr. Herman Dooyeweerd introduced the concept of a "religious ground motive" (RGM). According to Dooyeweerd, every philosophy is anchored in a core belief or commitment, religious or otherwise, that shapes how people view the world. This foundational idea influences how societies interact with reality and determine values, ethics, and truth. This chapter explores three major religious ground motives: the Christian RGM, the Modernist RGM, and the Postmodern RGM. Each of these perspectives offers distinct approaches to understanding life, society, and human flourishing.

## The Christian Philosophy Ground Motive

Dooyeweerd's Christian philosophy revolves around three key biblical themes: creation, the Fall, and redemption through Jesus Christ. It emphasizes that God is sovereign over all creation and has given it order and purpose. The Fall disrupted this divine order, but Christ's redemption provides a path to restore what was lost. This Christian RGM integrates faith with every aspect of life, asserting that all areas of human existence—whether scientific, social, or cultural—must be understood through the lens of God's creative and redemptive work.

### Biblical Foundation

The Christian RGM is grounded in Scriptures like Acts 17:28: "In him, we live and move and have our being" (WEB). This underscores the belief that life and reality are centered in Christ, influencing every dimension of existence.

## The Modernist Ground Motive

The Modernist RGM emerged during the Enlightenment, separating nature and grace, faith from reason. It places strong emphasis on human autonomy and the power of reason to discover truth. In this view, science, logic, and rationality are the primary tools for understanding the world, while religion is often relegated to the private sphere. Modernism values objectivity and the human capacity to shape the world through knowledge, often dismissing divine intervention or revelation.

### Philosophical Expression

René Descartes famously declared, "I think, therefore I am," which encapsulates Modernism's belief in human reason as the ultimate source of truth. In this framework, human thought is the foundation for understanding reality, often sidelining or ignoring the role of God.

# The Postmodern Ground Motive

Postmodernism, emerging as a critique of Modernism, rejects the notion of universal truths. It argues that all knowledge is subjective, shaped by culture, language, and power structures. Postmodern thinkers question the validity of grand narratives—stories or explanations that claim to offer universal truth—and instead focus on how individual and cultural experiences define what is "true" for different people. This skepticism of objective truth and emphasis on social context characterizes the Postmodern RGM.

### Cultural Critique

Jacques Derrida's statement, "There is nothing outside the text," reflects Postmodernism's claim that language shapes reality, and there is no absolute truth independent of interpretation. This has led to a worldview where truth is seen as fluid, based on individual or societal perception.

## Conflicts Among These Perspectives

### Truth and Objectivity

Christian philosophy upholds absolute truth as revealed by God, while Modernism seeks objective truth through human reason and science. Postmodernism, on the other hand, denies absolute truth altogether, asserting that all truths are relative to cultural or personal contexts.

### Authority and Knowledge

For Christians, God's revelation is the ultimate authority. Modernism places its trust in human reason and empirical evidence, while Postmodernism views knowledge as fragmented and dispersed among social and cultural groups, with no single source of authority.

### Purpose and Ethics

Christian philosophy grounds ethics and purpose in God's design for humanity, while Modernism takes a utilitarian approach, focusing on what is effective for human well-being. Postmodernism relativizes ethics, suggesting that what is considered "good" or "right" depends on individual or cultural perspectives.

## Surveying the History of Social Sciences Through Ground Motives

### Christian Philosophy and Early Social Sciences

In the early stages, social sciences were intertwined with Christian thought. During the Renaissance and Reformation, figures like the Scholastics engaged with social and economic issues through a theological lens, discussing justice, fairness, and the role of divine guidance in human affairs. Early psychology, too, was informed by Christian concepts of the soul, as the word "psychology" literally means "study of the soul." These disciplines sought to understand humanity in relation to God's design.

## The Rise of Modernism in Social Sciences

With the Enlightenment came a shift toward reason and science as the dominant forces in the social sciences. Figures like Auguste Comte, who coined the term "sociology," promoted the idea that human behavior and society could be studied objectively, using methods similar to those in the natural sciences. Religion was increasingly viewed as personal and irrelevant to scientific inquiry, with fields like psychology and economics seeking to uncover universal laws of human behavior.

## Postmodern Critiques in Social Sciences

Postmodernism disrupted the confidence of Modernism by arguing that social realities are too complex for universal laws. Thinkers like Michel Foucault explored how language, power, and societal structures shape human behavior and knowledge. Postmodernism opened up social sciences to multiple perspectives, encouraging a focus on marginalized voices and questioning whether objective knowledge is even possible.

# Conflicts and Synthesis in Social Sciences

### Objective vs. Subjective Knowledge

Modernism seeks to find objective truths, while Postmodernism claims all knowledge is subjective. Christian philosophy, however, teaches that objective truth is revealed by God and experienced personally, offering a middle ground between these two extremes.

### Values in Science

While Modernism claims to pursue value-neutral science, Christian philosophy insists that moral values are inherent in the pursuit of truth. Postmodernism critiques the supposed neutrality of science, arguing that cultural biases influence all knowledge, even scientific discovery.

### Human Nature

Christian philosophy teaches that humans are created by God, fallen due to sin, but redeemable through Christ. Modernism views humans as rational beings to be understood through science, while Postmodernism sees human identity as shaped entirely by social, cultural, and historical factors.

# Common Ground: Improving the Human Condition

Despite their differences, both Ministry Sciences and Social Sciences aim to improve human life. Social sciences focus on mental health, social justice, and economic development, while Ministry Sciences provide spiritual care and moral guidance. Both disciplines seek to help people thrive, though their approaches and underlying beliefs differ.

**Providing Support and Interventions**

Social Sciences use practical interventions to address societal problems like poverty and mental health issues. Ministry Sciences, however, offer spiritual counseling, coaching, and pastoral care integrating biblical wisdom with practical solutions.

**Promoting Societal Justice and Ethical Living**

Both Ministry Sciences and Social Sciences care deeply about justice and ethical living. Social scientists work on human rights and social equity, while Ministry Sciences focus on biblical teachings about compassion, fairness, and love for others.

## Differences Between Ministry Sciences and Modernist Social Sciences

The key difference lies in how God is viewed in human life. Modernist Social Sciences often exclude God from their framework, focusing solely on human behavior and societal patterns. Ministry Sciences, however, invite God into every area of life, using biblical principles alongside scientific tools to support human flourishing.

## Ministry Sciences and Postmodern Social Sciences

Ministry Sciences and Postmodernism diverge sharply. Postmodernism denies universal truths, favoring relative and context-specific interpretations of reality. Ministry Sciences affirm the existence of absolute truth revealed by God. While Postmodernism deconstructs traditional beliefs, Ministry Sciences uphold the authority of Scripture as the ultimate guide for human life.

## Conclusion: A Call to Action

Ministry Sciences offer a path that integrates faith, reason, and practical care to improve human life. By understanding the competing ground motives—Christian, Modernist, and Postmodern—we gain insight into how different worldviews shape our understanding of the world. As Christians, we are called to engage with these perspectives and explore how God has uniquely gifted and called each of us to serve in ministry.

# Different Philosophies for Flourishing

**Understanding Religious Ground Motives: Christian, Modernist, and Postmodern Perspectives**

# Introduction

When I graduated from Dordt College (now Dordt University) with a degree in philosophy in 1983, many wondered what I could do with such a degree besides ministry. Over the years, I've realized how valuable my Christian philosophy degree has been in shaping how I think about ministry. Christian philosophy, especially the work of Dr. Herman Dooyeweerd and Dr. Roy Clouser, has shown how religious beliefs influence all areas of thought, including social sciences. Ministry Sciences is built on the foundational work of these Christian philosophers. Here's how Dooyeweerd and Clouser have significantly contributed to Ministry Sciences.

# Dr. Herman Dooyeweerd: Architect of Reformational Philosophy

## Background and Contributions

Dr. Herman Dooyeweerd (1894–1977) was a Dutch philosopher known for his "Reformational philosophy," which integrates a Christian worldview into philosophical thinking. He taught at the Free University of Amsterdam and played a key role in the Reformational movement.

## The Religious Ground Motive

At the center of Dooyeweerd's philosophy is the idea of a "religious ground motive." He believed every philosophy is driven by a core religious or spiritual belief that shapes its view of reality. He identified four key religious ground motives that have shaped Western thought:

1. **Form-Matter Motive**: From ancient Greek philosophy, this reflects the split between eternal, unchanging ideas (forms) and the physical, changing world (matter). Plato and Aristotle were influenced by this.
2. **Nature-Grace Motive**: In the Middle Ages, there was a tension between the natural world and divine grace. This was central in medieval Christian thought, especially in the works of Thomas Aquinas.
3. **Nature-Freedom Motive**: This motive became important during the Enlightenment, where philosophers like Kant and Rousseau focused on the tension between natural laws and human freedom.
4. **Creation-Fall-Redemption Motive**: Dooyeweerd believed this is the true biblical view. It sees reality through the biblical story of creation, the fall, and redemption. It shows how everything in life is connected under God's rule, recognizing the effects of sin and the redemptive power of Christ.

## Scriptural Foundation

This creation-fall-redemption framework is based on several key Bible passages:

- **Creation**: "In the beginning, God created the heavens and the earth." (Genesis 1:1, WEB)
- **Fall**: "Sin entered into the world through one man, and death through sin; and so death passed to all men, because all sinned." (Romans 5:12, WEB)

- **Redemption**: "He has rescued us from the power of darkness and brought us into the Kingdom of the Son he loves." (Colossians 1:13-14, WEB)

**Impact on Ministry Sciences**

Dooyeweerd's philosophy impacts Ministry Sciences in these key ways:

- **Holistic Approach**: The creation-fall-redemption motive helps ministries see all aspects of life—spiritual, social, and physical—as connected under God's rule. This influences how ministries address issues like poverty, injustice, and spiritual growth.
- **Worldview Analysis**: Understanding the religious ground motives helps ministers engage with the beliefs that shape the people they serve. This is crucial for developing effective ministry strategies.
- **Cultural Engagement**: Knowing how different ground motives have influenced history helps ministry leaders engage with culture thoughtfully, challenging ideas that conflict with a biblical worldview.

## Dr. Roy Clouser: Revealing the Role of Faith in Knowledge

**Background and Contributions**

Dr. Roy Clouser is an American philosopher known for his work on the relationship between faith and reason. His book *The Myth of Religious Neutrality* argues that all theories, whether religious or secular, are shaped by underlying religious beliefs.

**The Religious Ground Motive**

Clouser builds on Dooyeweerd's ideas, emphasizing that no human thought is neutral. He believes every belief system, even those that claim to be purely scientific or secular, is based on religious commitments that shape how people understand the world.

**Key Themes in Clouser's Thought**

1. **No Neutrality**: Clouser argues that the idea of an unbiased perspective is a myth. Every person and theory operates from a faith-based commitment, whether it's faith in God or something else.

    - *Scriptural Support*: "For as he thinks within himself, so is he." (Proverbs 23:7, WEB)
2. **Biblical Worldview**: Clouser stresses the importance of a worldview grounded in the Bible, acknowledging God's rule over all of life.

    - *Scriptural Support*: "Your word is a lamp to my feet, and a light for my path." (Psalm 119:105, WEB)
3. **Faith and Reason Together**: Clouser rejects the idea that faith and reason are separate.

Instead, he says faith is the foundation of all rational thought.

- ○ *Scriptural Support*: "Trust in Yahweh with all your heart, and don't lean on your own understanding." (Proverbs 3:5-6, WEB)

**Impact on Ministry Sciences**

Clouser's philosophy is important for Ministry Sciences in these ways:

- **Critical Thinking**: Recognizing that all ideas are influenced by faith commitments helps ministry leaders think critically about the assumptions behind various cultural ideas.
- **Biblical Foundation**: Clouser's focus on the Bible helps ministries stay rooted in Scripture while engaging with modern challenges.
- **Integration of Knowledge**: Understanding the relationship between faith and reason helps ministry leaders deal with complex issues in areas like counseling, pastoral care, and coaching ministry.

## The Modernist Religious Ground Motive

The Modernist religious ground motive began during the Enlightenment, a period in the 17th and 18th centuries that emphasized human reason, science, and progress. It has three main features:

1. **Nature vs. Grace**: Modernism separates the natural world (explained by science and reason) from grace (religion and faith), seeing them as unrelated.
2. **Human Autonomy**: Modernism focuses on human autonomy, where people use reason to understand the world and make moral choices, often disregarding the need for God.
3. **Science as Truth**: Modernism believes that science and reason are the best ways to discover truth, often sidelining religious or spiritual views.

**Impact of Modernism**

- **Compartmentalization**: This division between nature and grace leads people to separate faith from reason. For example, someone might approach their work scientifically but keep their faith private.
- **Faith vs. Reason**: Modernism often creates conflict between science and religion, such as in debates over evolution.

## The Postmodern Religious Ground Motive

Postmodernism arose in response to Modernism's confidence in science and reason. It's characterized by skepticism, relativism, and the rejection of universal truths. Postmodernism challenges the big stories of history, religion, and science, promoting a pluralistic view of truth.

**Key Ideas of Postmodernism**

1. **Skepticism and Relativism**: Postmodernism questions the idea of absolute truth,

believing that what we call "truth" is shaped by culture and language.
2   **Rejection of Grand Narratives**: Postmodernism rejects big stories that claim to explain everything, instead embracing multiple perspectives.
3   **Language and Power**: Postmodernism sees language as shaping reality and believes that knowledge is influenced by power dynamics.

**Paul on Mars Hill: A Biblical Response to Postmodernism**

The Apostle Paul's approach to the philosophers in Athens, as recorded in Acts 17:16-34, offers a biblical model for engaging with postmodern thinking.

- **Engagement with Beliefs**: Paul respected the Athenians' religious practices and found common ground by referring to their altar to an unknown god.
- **Challenging Narratives**: He challenged their views by introducing the idea of a transcendent God who created everything.

## Christian Tradition and Advocacy for the Marginalized

While postmodernism claims to advocate for the marginalized, this role has long been part of Christian tradition. Jesus and the early church championed the poor, women, and the outcast.

- **Jesus' Ministry**: Jesus reached out to marginalized people like the Samaritan woman at the well and empowered women in His ministry.
- **The Early Church**: Early Christians cared for the sick, the poor, and those rejected by society, continuing Jesus' example.

## Conclusion

Dr. Herman Dooyeweerd and Dr. Roy Clouser have helped lay the foundation for Ministry Sciences by showing how religious beliefs shape all areas of life. Understanding the Christian, Modernist, and Postmodern ground motives helps us better engage with the world today. Ministry Sciences builds on these insights, continuing the Christian tradition of advocating for the marginalized and helping people see the world through the lens of faith in God.

**Books for Further Reading:**

- *The Myth of Religious Neutrality* by Roy Clouser
- *A New Critique of Theoretical Thought* by Herman Dooyeweerd
- *The Enlightenment: The Pursuit of Happiness 1680-1790* by Ritchie Robertson
- *Explaining Postmodernism* by Stephen R.C. Hicks

# Religious Ground Motive of Ministry Sciences

## Ministry Sciences with the Christian Religious Ground Motive

We've looked at the religious ground motives of Christian Philosophy, Modernism, and Postmodernism. Later, we'll touch on Metamodernism, which mixes ideas from both Modernism and Postmodernism.

### Overview of Religious Ground Motives

In the next few chapters, we will explore how different religious ground motives influence Ministry Sciences, Modern Social Sciences, Postmodern Social Sciences, and Metamodernism Social Sciences. These chapters will help compare these four approaches.

## Ministry Sciences and the Christian Religious Ground Motive

Ministry Sciences is built on the Christian Religious Ground Motive (RGM), which is based on the work and teachings of Jesus Christ, as revealed in the Bible. Both the Old and New Testaments provide the foundation for Ministry Sciences, which looks at all knowledge through the lens of Scripture.

In Ministry Sciences, God is involved in every part of life, guiding people toward healing, transformation, and wholeness because they are made in His image.

### How the Religious Ground Motive Shapes Ministry Sciences

In Ministry Sciences, the Religious Ground Motive is based on the Bible and Christianity. Nothing here will surprise you if you're familiar with Christian teachings. To understand how Ministry Sciences fits into this bigger picture, let's look at some key topics and fields of study:

- **Theology**: The study of God, religious beliefs, and how we practice faith.
- **Comparative Religion**: Comparing different religions to find similarities and differences.
- **History of Religion**: Learning how religions have changed and developed over time.
- **Philosophy of Religion**: Thinking deeply about religious ideas and beliefs, such as the existence of God and the problem of evil.
- **Sociology of Religion**: Studying how religion interacts with society and influences behavior.
- **Psychology of Religion**: Looking at how religious beliefs shape our minds and mental health.
- **Religious Ethics**: Studying how religious beliefs guide moral decisions.
- **Religious Practices and Rituals**: Exploring religious ceremonies and rituals and their

meanings.
- **Sacred Texts**: Studying and interpreting religious writings.

This book will briefly touch on each of these areas, comparing how Ministry Sciences, Modernism, Postmodernism, and Metamodernism approach these topics.

## Christianity and Ministry Sciences

Ministry Sciences is based on Christianity and the Bible's core beliefs of Creation, Fall, and Redemption. It also aligns with important Christian creeds and beliefs.

### Key Figures in Christianity

Christianity is rooted in the belief that God created the world, as described in Genesis 1-2. Humans were placed in the Garden of Eden and given a choice to follow God's commands or go their own way, which led to the fall into sin (Genesis 2-3). Throughout the Old Testament, we see examples of people either following God or turning away from Him. These stories of prophets, priests, and kings help us understand how humans relate to God. While the Old Testament is rooted in history, its teachings are timeless and continue to shape Ministry Sciences.

In the New Testament, the story of Jesus Christ—the central figure in history—fulfills the promises of the Old Testament. Jesus' birth, ministry, sacrifice, victory over death, and promise of His return are key to the Christian faith. The Christian ground motive of creation, fall, and redemption fully reveals itself through Jesus.

### Foundational Creed: The Apostles' Creed

The **Apostles' Creed** is a basic summary of Christian beliefs. It comes from the teachings of the apostles and is a unifying statement of faith for different Christian groups. It explains key beliefs about God, Jesus, and the Holy Spirit and emphasizes core doctrines like resurrection and eternal life.

## The Apostles' Creed

I believe in God, the Father Almighty,
Creator of heaven and earth,
And in Jesus Christ, His only Son, our Lord,
Who was conceived by the Holy Spirit,
Born of the Virgin Mary,
Suffered under Pontius Pilate,
Was crucified, died, and was buried;
He descended to the dead.
On the third day, He rose again;

He ascended into heaven,
And is seated at the right hand of God the Father Almighty.
From there He will come to judge the living and the dead.

I believe in the Holy Spirit,
The holy catholic Church,
The communion of saints,
The forgiveness of sins,
The resurrection of the body,
And life everlasting. Amen.

## The Ministry Sciences Creed

The Ministry Sciences Creed builds on traditional Christian beliefs, focusing on how ministry connects people to God and how scientific inquiry can help us understand God's creation. It also highlights that humans are both spiritual and physical beings made in the image of God.

**Ministry Sciences Creed**

- **We believe in the connection with God through the study of ministry, using biblical, theological, and philosophical approaches** (2 Timothy 3:16-17; Colossians 2:8).

- **We believe in God, the Creator, who reveals Himself through Scripture and nature** (Romans 1:20; Genesis 1:1). Humans are made in His image, as spiritual and physical beings (Genesis 2:7; 1 Corinthians 15:45).

- **We affirm the partnership of male and female**, who were created to complement each other and work together (Genesis 2:18). This partnership honors God in work, marriage, and family (Ecclesiastes 4:9-12; 1 Corinthians 7:7-9).

- **We believe that marriage is a lifelong commitment between one man and one woman**, reflecting God's design for love and faithfulness (Matthew 19:4-6). Ministry Sciences supports a strong, loving marriage, where sexual expression is cherished (1 Corinthians 7:3-5). Christian marriage is also the best place for raising children (Ephesians 6:4).

- **We recognize the importance of single parents** and their role in raising children (James 1:27).

- **We believe in scientific inquiry as a way to understand God's creation** and see His handiwork in the world (Psalm 19:1-2; Romans 1:20).

- **We believe in the Bible as the inspired Word of God** (2 Timothy 3:16-17). The Bible's message is confirmed by historical evidence, like the resurrection of Jesus Christ (1 Corinthians 15:3-4).

- **We believe Adam and Eve's sin introduced brokenness into the world**, and because of their choice, all of creation needs redemption (Romans 3:23; Genesis 3).

- **We believe in Jesus Christ as the Savior and Redeemer**, who offers new life through His resurrection (John 3:16-17; 1 Peter 1:3).

- **We believe in the Holy Spirit**, who gives us gifts, guides us, and helps us grow in Christ (Acts 1:8; Galatians 5:22-23).

- **We believe God calls Christians to share the gospel with others** and bring them back to Him (Matthew 28:19-20).

- **We believe in training and equipping ministers** to lead others to Christ (Ephesians 4:11-12).

This creed aligns with the biblical truths found in Genesis and the Gospel of John, which describe the creation of humanity in God's image, the fall into sin, and the hope of redemption through Jesus Christ.

### Biblical Foundations: Genesis and John

The Ministry Sciences Creed is deeply connected to the biblical stories found in **Genesis** and **John**, which show how God created the world, humans fell into sin, and Jesus Christ came to redeem us.

In Genesis 1 and 2, God created the heavens and the earth, and in Genesis 3, Adam and Eve's disobedience led to the fall. In the **Gospel of John**, we see the fulfillment of God's redemption plan through Jesus, who is the "Word" that became flesh and brought salvation to the world (John 1:1-14).

## Conclusion

Ministry Sciences is firmly rooted in the Christian religious ground motive, focusing on the biblical story of creation, fall, and redemption. By building on key Christian beliefs and connecting them to ministry, we aim to equip Christian leaders to serve God's purpose in the world. This approach highlights the importance of biblical teaching, training leaders, and spreading the hope of Christ's redemption to others.

# Modernist Religious Ground Motive

## Modernist Social Sciences: A Hidden Belief System

### Introduction

When we think about belief systems, we usually think of religions like Christianity, Islam, or Judaism. But what if I told you that **Modernist Social Sciences**, even though they claim to be purely scientific, act like a religion of their own? They have sacred texts, professional leaders like therapists and counselors, and even their own doctrines. For Christians, it's important to recognize that while Modernist Social Sciences may not speak about God, they still promote their own worldview—a worldview that often contradicts biblical truth.

This chapter explores how Modernist Social Sciences function as a belief system, their "sacred texts," their goals for human life, and how Christians can think critically about them.

### The "Sacred Texts" of Modernist Social Sciences

Just like Christianity is grounded in the Bible, Modernist Social Sciences have foundational books written by influential thinkers. These books, while based on scientific research, are treated as guides for how we should think about human nature, behavior, and society.

Some of the most important "sacred texts" include:

- **Sigmund Freud's "The Interpretation of Dreams"**: Freud's ideas about the unconscious mind and how our childhood experiences shape us laid the foundation for modern psychoanalysis. While Freud's work is popular in psychology, it often opposes Christian views of human nature, especially regarding sin and moral responsibility.

- **B.F. Skinner's "Beyond Freedom and Dignity"**: Skinner believed that our behavior is determined by our environment. His work on behaviorism claims that humans can be shaped and controlled through rewards and punishments. But as Christians, we know that human beings are more than just products of their surroundings—we have free will, created in the image of God.

- **Jean Piaget's "The Origins of Intelligence in Children"**: Piaget's research on child development influences how schools and psychologists understand the way children grow and learn. While his theories are valuable, they often leave out the spiritual development that comes from knowing God and learning biblical truths.

These texts serve as the foundation for how Modernist Social Sciences approach the human condition, but for Christians, we know that without God's truth, these explanations are incomplete.

## The Goals of Modernist Social Sciences

Modernist Social Sciences aim to improve human life, but their vision of what that looks like is very different from the Christian understanding of human flourishing. For them, the focus is on personal happiness, ethical living based on human reasoning, and creating a fairer society—without acknowledging God's role in any of it.

Let's explore their main goals:

- **Human Flourishing**: Modernist Social Sciences want to help people live happy, healthy lives through therapy, education, and social policies. While this seems good on the surface, their definition of flourishing often leaves out the most important part—**our relationship with God**. True human flourishing can only be found in Christ, not in human efforts alone.

- **Ethical Living**: They focus on how people develop morals, often based on thinkers like Lawrence Kohlberg, who studied how humans learn right from wrong. But unlike Christians, who believe that morality comes from God, Modernist Social Sciences often base their ethics on human reasoning, which can change over time.

- **Social Harmony**: They work to solve issues like inequality and discrimination to make society more just. While Christians are also called to seek justice and love our neighbors, we know that real peace and justice come only through the redemption and grace found in Christ, not through human efforts alone.

## The Leaders of Modernist Social Sciences: Therapists and Counselors

In Christianity, pastors and church leaders guide people in their spiritual lives. In the world of Modernist Social Sciences, the "leaders" are therapists, counselors, and social workers. These professionals help people with personal struggles, offering emotional and psychological guidance, much like how a pastor might offer spiritual guidance.

But there's a key difference: while Christian leaders point people toward God's truth, many therapists and counselors in Modernist Social Sciences leave God out of the conversation. They offer solutions that focus only on human abilities, missing out on the deeper healing that only comes through Jesus Christ.

## The "Church" of Modernist Social Sciences

If we think of the Modernist Social Sciences as a belief system, it's not too hard to see how they resemble a "church." Like a church, they have important texts, respected leaders, and a community of professionals who share the same beliefs. Here are some similarities:

- **Doctrines**: Just as Christians follow biblical doctrines, Modernist Social Sciences follow the ideas and theories of thinkers like Freud, Skinner, and Piaget. These theories are taught in universities, published in journals, and passed down through training programs.

- **Community**: Therapists, counselors, and other professionals form communities much like churches do. They belong to professional organizations, attend conferences, and learn from one another, much like how Christians gather for fellowship and teaching.

- **Rituals**: Certifications, degrees, and continuing education workshops act as the "rituals" of this system. They mark the progress and commitment of the people involved, much like how baptisms or ordinations mark important spiritual milestones in the church.

## The Beliefs of Modernist Social Sciences

While Modernist Social Sciences don't claim to have a creed like Christianity, they do promote certain beliefs that often contradict Christian teaching. Here's a simplified version of their "creed":

1 **We do not believe in God or spiritual matters**. (Bertrand Russell)

2 **We believe in evolution and natural selection as the explanations for life**. (Charles Darwin)

3 **We trust science and evidence to find the truth, not divine revelation**. (Karl Popper)

4 **Humans create their own meaning in life, not based on any divine purpose**. (Sigmund Freud)

5 **Our focus is on improving life here and now, not on an afterlife**. (Richard Dawkins)

6 **We base morality on human reason and evidence, not on religious teachings**. (Jeremy Bentham)

7 **We believe that psychology and social sciences can help us better understand human behavior and improve society**. (Émile Durkheim)

For Christians, this worldview is missing the most crucial element: **God's truth**. While science can help us understand the world, we know that true wisdom comes from God. The Bible tells us that "the fear of the Lord is the beginning of wisdom" (Proverbs 9:10), something Modernist Social Sciences ignore.

## Conclusion: A Hidden Belief System

It's clear that Modernist Social Sciences, despite claiming to be neutral, function much like a belief system or religion. They have their own doctrines, leaders, and practices, and they promote a worldview that often contradicts the biblical truth we hold dear as Christians. Understanding this can help us, as believers, to critically engage with these ideas, using the Bible as our guide.

As Christians, we can appreciate the helpful insights that Modernist Social Sciences bring, but we must always remember that true healing, understanding, and flourishing come only through our relationship with God. Jesus said, "I am the way, and the truth, and the life" (John 14:6), and that's the ultimate truth we must hold onto, no matter what any human system might claim.

**For Further Reading:**

- *The God Who Is There* by Francis A. Schaeffer
- *The Myth of Religious Neutrality* by Roy A. Clouser
- *Desiring the Kingdom* by James K.A. Smith
- *Ideas Have Consequences* by Richard M. Weaver

# Postmodern Religous Belief Motive

## Postmodern Social Sciences: A Belief System of Its Own

### Introduction

What happens when society decides that there's no ultimate truth, no clear design from God, and no higher authority? That's where **Postmodern Social Sciences** come in—a system that says everyone can create their own truth, and that reality is whatever we decide it is. Even though they claim to be based on facts, the way Postmodern Social Sciences operate is like a religion. They have their own "sacred texts," religious goals, and even their own "clergy" in the form of therapists and counselors.

In this chapter, we'll explore how Postmodern Social Sciences work as a belief system, with foundational books, key goals, and leaders who guide people through life's challenges. As Christians, it's important to recognize this hidden belief system and understand how it shapes today's culture.

### The "Sacred Texts" of Postmodern Social Sciences

Just as Christianity is rooted in the Bible, Postmodern Social Sciences are built on important works written by thinkers who challenge traditional views of truth, power, and identity. These "sacred texts" shape how people view themselves and the world around them, even though they leave God out of the picture.

**Key texts and their influence include:**

- **Michel Foucault's "Discipline and Punish"**: Foucault looks at how society controls people through rules, institutions, and power structures. This book is foundational for understanding how modern society shapes people's behavior and identities. But for Christians, we know that true freedom and identity come from being children of God, not from breaking free of societal norms.

- **Judith Butler's "Gender Trouble"**: Butler argues that gender isn't something we're born with but something we perform based on social expectations. This idea has had a huge impact on gender and queer studies, but it directly challenges the biblical understanding that God created us male and female, with a clear design and purpose (Genesis 1:27).

- **Jean-François Lyotard's "The Postmodern Condition"**: Lyotard explains that in postmodern society, people no longer believe in grand narratives—big stories that explain everything, like Christianity. Instead, people believe in small, personal truths that change from one person to another. This completely opposes the Christian belief that God's truth is eternal and unchanging.

These books act as the foundation for Postmodern Social Sciences, shaping how people think about power, identity, and reality. But without God, these explanations can lead to confusion and uncertainty about what's truly right and wrong.

**The Religious Goals of Postmodern Social Sciences**

Every belief system has its goals, and Postmodern Social Sciences are no different. Their mission is to tear down what they see as oppressive structures, redefine identity, and create a society where everyone's personal truth is accepted. Here's what that looks like:

- **Breaking Down Power Structures**: Postmodern Social Sciences want to expose and dismantle what they see as systems of control—whether that's government, the church, or social norms. For example, Michel Foucault's ideas about how institutions control people are widely used to challenge traditional Christian morals.

- **Redefining Identity**: Judith Butler's work, for instance, argues that identity—especially gender—is not fixed but something we create. While this appeals to those who feel trapped by traditional roles, it contradicts the biblical teaching that our identity is given by God and that we are fearfully and wonderfully made (Psalm 139:14).

- **Creating an Inclusive Society**: Postmodernists aim to build a world where every individual is free to define their truth and live according to it. On the surface, this seems positive, but the lack of moral absolutes often leads to confusion and division, rather than the unity and love we find in Christ (1 Corinthians 1:10).

**The "Clergy" of Postmodern Social Sciences: Therapists and Counselors**

In Christianity, pastors and church leaders guide people in their spiritual lives. In the world of Postmodern Social Sciences, the "clergy" are therapists and counselors. These professionals help people navigate personal challenges, offering emotional support and helping them "discover" their own truth, much like how pastors help people discover God's truth.

But there's a major difference: Christian leaders point people toward the unchanging truth found in Jesus. In contrast, many therapists in Postmodern Social Sciences encourage individuals to create their own reality, which can lead people further from God's design and the truth of His Word.

### The "Church" of Postmodern Social Sciences

Even though Postmodern Social Sciences don't call themselves a religion, they have many things in common with organized belief systems. They have key texts, respected leaders, and a community of people who share the same beliefs. Here's what their "church" looks like:

- **Following the Doctrine**: Just like Christians follow biblical teachings, Postmodern Social Sciences follow the ideas of thinkers like Foucault, Butler, and Lyotard. These doctrines are taught in universities, written about in academic papers, and practiced by professionals in the field.

- **Community and Belonging**: Therapists, counselors, and academics who follow Postmodern Social Sciences gather at conferences, join professional organizations, and work together to promote their beliefs, much like how Christians gather for fellowship.

- **Rituals and Ceremonies**: Just as Christians celebrate baptisms and ordinations, Postmodern Social Sciences have their own rituals—like graduations, certifications, and workshops—that mark important stages in a person's career or development in their belief system.

### Religious Gatherings: Celebrations of Identity and Diversity

One of the clearest examples of how Postmodern Social Sciences function like a belief system is seen in events like **Pride celebrations**. These events are more than just social gatherings—they're like religious festivals that celebrate personal identity and diversity. For participants, these events offer a sense of belonging, affirmation, and spiritual connection.

**Pride events**: Each year, LGBTQ+ individuals and their allies come together to celebrate identity, advocate for rights, and build a sense of community. These events often include parades, speeches, performances, and activism. For many, it's a public declaration of their belief in the Postmodern idea that people can define their own identity.

For Christians, this stands in contrast to the biblical belief that our identity is defined by God, not by culture or personal feelings (Galatians 3:28).

# The Creed of Postmodern Social Sciences

Here's what the core beliefs of Postmodern Social Sciences might look like, if they were written out as a creed:

1. **We do not believe in God or any divine design.** (Michel Foucault)

2. **We believe that language shapes reality, and each person creates their own truth.** (Judith Butler)

3. **We reject all grand narratives and aim to deconstruct them.** (Jean-François Lyotard)

4. **There are no absolutes—except the belief that there are no absolutes.** (Richard Rorty)

5. **Our goal is to cope with life as best we can, without the hope of eternal life.** (Michel Foucault)

6. **We believe in supporting those marginalized by traditional views of truth and reality.** (Eve Kosofsky Sedgwick)

7. **We find salvation in transforming identities, not through faith in God, but through the freedom to define ourselves.** (Judith Butler)

## Conclusion: A Hidden Belief System

Postmodern Social Sciences claim to be neutral, but they function much like a religious system. They have sacred texts, religious leaders, and a clear set of beliefs that shape how people view themselves and the world. As Christians, we need to be aware of this hidden belief system and the ways it challenges the truth of God's Word.

By understanding the beliefs behind Postmodern Social Sciences, we can better engage with them from a Christian perspective. We know that true identity, freedom, and hope are found in Jesus Christ, not in redefining reality to suit our desires. Jesus said, "You will know the truth, and the truth will set you free" (John 8:32), and that's the truth we must hold onto.

## For Further Reading:

- *Truth Decay: Defending Christianity Against the Challenges of Postmodernism* by Douglas Groothuis
- *The Supremacy of Christ in a Postmodern World* edited by John Piper and Justin Taylor
- *Postmodern Times: A Christian Guide to Contemporary Thought and Culture* by Gene Edward Veith Jr.
- *The Death of Truth* by David F. Wells

# Metamodernism as a Religious Ground Motive

## Metamodernism as a Religious System

### Introduction

Have you ever met someone who seems to believe one thing today and something totally different tomorrow? That's a bit like **Metamodernism**, a new cultural and philosophical movement that embraces contradictions and shifts between perspectives. One day, a metamodernist might sound like an enthusiastic modernist, full of optimism about science and progress. The next day, they might sound like a postmodernist, full of irony and doubt. They're like someone standing on a bridge, leaning from one side to the other—never fully committing to either.

Many **social media influencers**, **artists**, **movie storytellers**, and **philosophers** consider themselves metamodernists. They love to quote both the modernists and the postmodernists, switching sides depending on what's useful for the moment. Metamodernism is becoming more influential in culture, and as Christians, it's important to understand what it is, how it functions like a religion, and how it challenges our faith.

### The Religious Ground Motive of Metamodernism

At its core, **Metamodernism** is all about *oscillation*—swinging between extremes. It goes back and forth between modernism, with its belief in progress and science, and postmodernism, which rejects absolute truth and embraces skepticism.

- **Modernism** believes humanity can make the world better through science, reason, and universal truths.
- **Postmodernism** says there are no universal truths and that all knowledge is relative— what's true for you might not be true for me.

Metamodernists accept both ideas, even though they contradict each other. They acknowledge that Postmodernism's skepticism has its limits but still appreciate Modernism's hope for progress. So, they bounce between conviction and doubt, between sincerity and irony. It's like they can't decide which side to land on, so they live in the tension between the two. As Christians, we understand this tension, but we believe that the truth doesn't change. God's Word is eternal and stands firm, no matter how culture shifts (Isaiah 40:8).

### Sacred Texts and Influential Works of Metamodernism

Just as Christians have the Bible, Metamodernism has its own set of "sacred texts"—books, movies, and cultural works that shape its beliefs and practices. These influential works help people understand how to navigate the constant shifting between hope and doubt, order and chaos.

**Key texts and their influence include:**

- **"Notes on Metamodernism" by Timotheus Vermeulen and Robin van den Akker**: This is like the "Bible" of Metamodernism, introducing the idea of oscillation between modernist and postmodernist thinking. It sets the stage for how metamodernists see the world.

- **"Metamodernism: The Future of Theory" by Seth Abramson**: Abramson's book dives deeper into the theory behind Metamodernism. It's foundational for those who want to understand the cultural and philosophical ideas driving this movement.

- **Shia LaBeouf's "Just Do It" Performance**: Believe it or not, the actor Shia LaBeouf is considered a metamodernist thinker. His viral performance art, where he screams "Just do it!" in a mix of sincerity and irony, captures the emotional and intellectual complexity of Metamodernism.

These texts guide people on how to move between hope and doubt, sincerity and irony, as if they're on a never-ending journey without a fixed destination. But as Christians, we know that God provides us with a clear destination—His kingdom—and a steady path to follow (Matthew 7:13-14).

**The Creed of Metamodernism**

If Metamodernism had a creed, it might look something like this:

1 **We believe in the constant swing between sincerity and irony, embracing both hope and doubt** (Timotheus Vermeulen and Robin van den Akker).

2 **We believe in the power of stories, whether they are big, universal stories or small, personal ones, to shape how we understand the world** (Seth Abramson).

3 **We believe in blending deep emotions with intellectual critique to create a fuller human experience** (Shia LaBeouf).

4 **We believe that multiple truths can coexist, and reality is complex and often contradictory** (Timotheus Vermeulen).

5 **We believe in the potential for social and cultural renewal, fueled by a balance of optimism and skepticism**(Robin van den Akker).

6 **We believe in empathy, collaboration, and the importance of addressing global challenges together** (Seth Abramson).

7 **We believe that art and culture have the power to change the world** (Shia LaBeouf).

**8    We believe in respecting the past but always looking toward the future** (Timotheus Vermeulen).

This creed emphasizes fluidity and flexibility, but it lacks the solid foundation that Christians find in the Word of God. While Metamodernism embraces shifting ideas, Christianity teaches that "Jesus Christ is the same yesterday and today and forever" (Hebrews 13:8).

## The Goals of Metamodernism

Just like any belief system, Metamodernism has goals—objectives that its followers pursue through art, culture, and intellectual discussions. These goals are similar to the religious goals of personal growth, social harmony, and cultural transformation found in many faith traditions.

**Key goals include:**

- **Personal Growth**: Metamodernism encourages people to grow emotionally and intellectually by balancing their sincere feelings with critical thinking. It promotes self-awareness and resilience but often without a grounding in God's truth.

- **Social Harmony**: Metamodernists believe in fostering empathy and interconnectedness to address social issues like inequality and discrimination. While these goals align with Christian teachings to love your neighbor (Matthew 22:39), they often lack the deeper spiritual foundation of seeing every person as made in God's image.

- **Cultural Renewal**: Metamodernism emphasizes the power of art and culture to inspire change and challenge the status quo. This focus on creativity is important, but it often promotes messages that contradict biblical values.

## The "Clergy" of Metamodernism: Thought Leaders and Cultural Critics

In Christianity, pastors and church leaders guide believers in their walk with God. In the world of Metamodernism, **thought leaders, artists, writers, journalists, and cultural critics** act as the "clergy." These influencers help people navigate the complexities of modern life by encouraging them to embrace contradictions and live in a state of constant flux.

For example, a metamodernist thought leader might encourage people to believe in progress one day and question everything the next. But without a firm foundation in God's truth, this kind of guidance can lead people astray, leaving them confused and spiritually adrift.

## Elijah and the Prophets of Baal: A Reflection on Oscillation

The story of Elijah and the prophets of Baal in **1 Kings 18:20-39** offers a powerful biblical reflection on the dangers of constantly wavering between two sides. The people of Israel were torn between worshiping Yahweh and following the pagan god Baal. Elijah confronted them, saying, *"How long will you waver between two opinions? If the Lord is God, follow him; but if Baal is God, follow him"* (1 Kings 18:21).

This challenge is similar to what we see in Metamodernism today. Metamodernists waver between truth and doubt, between conviction and skepticism, much like the Israelites wavered between Yahweh and Baal. Elijah called the people to make a decision and commit to the one true God. In the same way, Christians are called to stand firm in their faith, rather than oscillating between the changing ideas of the world (Ephesians 4:14).

## Conclusion

Metamodernism functions like a religious system, with its own foundational texts, goals, and leaders. It encourages people to embrace contradictions, but in doing so, it leaves them without the solid foundation that comes from knowing God's eternal truth. As Christians, we are called to be grounded in the Word of God and to follow Jesus, who provides us with a clear and unwavering path.

By understanding the influence of Metamodernism, we can better engage with today's culture and offer the hope of the gospel—a hope that doesn't waver or oscillate, but stands firm in Christ (1 Corinthians 15:58).

**For Further Study:**

- *"Notes on Metamodernism"* by Timotheus Vermeulen and Robin van den Akker
- *"Metamodernism: The Future of Theory"* by Seth Abramson
- *"Infinite Jest"* by David Foster Wallace
- *"The Matrix and Philosophy: Welcome to the Desert of the Real"* edited by William Irwin
- *"Culture Care: Reconnecting with Beauty for Our Common Life"* by Makoto Fujimura
- *"After Virtue: A Study in Moral Theory"* by Alasdair MacIntyre

# Methodologies

## The Methodologies of Social Sciences and Ministry Sciences

### Historical Context

For centuries, **churches** have cared for people's emotional, psychological, and spiritual needs— long before modern psychology was even a thing. A great example is the **confessional booth** in churches, where people would confess their sins, share their burdens, and receive spiritual guidance. This helped unburden their souls and provided psychological relief in a way that acknowledged God's role in healing.

## The Evolution of Social Sciences

Believe it or not, the early roots of **social sciences** were closely linked to this Christian approach to soul care. The word "psychology" comes from the Greek word *psyche*, meaning "soul," and *logos*, meaning "study." It originally focused on the soul and was connected with Christian philosophy and theology. But as time passed, particularly during the **Enlightenment**, things changed. The rise of **Modernism** shifted the focus to science and reason, leaving the Christian worldview behind. Social sciences like **psychology**, **sociology**, and **economics** began to emerge as disciplines that tried to explain human behavior and societal patterns without God in the picture.

### Secularization of Soul Care

As **social scientists** started addressing mental health, social justice, and community issues, they often left out the role that faith and God play in people's lives. This sidelined the church's historical role in caring for souls. Today, social sciences offer solutions, but without recognizing the spiritual aspect of life that Christian ministries address.

### Holistic Approach to Human Well-Being

Both **social sciences** and **ministry sciences** aim to help people and improve society, but they approach it from completely different angles. Social sciences focus on community programs to tackle issues like poverty, addiction, and education, but they don't bring God into the equation.

In contrast, Christian ministries not only offer practical help, like counseling and support, but also bring **God** into every part of the process. Christian ministry is centered around hope found in a relationship with Jesus, which goes beyond just coping with life's struggles—it offers a deep, soul-healing hope rooted in eternal life. While Christian psychologists may integrate both science and faith, mainstream social sciences generally exclude the spiritual dimension from their methodologies.

## Methodologies in Social Sciences

### Modernist Social Sciences

**Modernist Social Sciences** focus on empirical, scientific methods to understand human behavior and community needs. This approach excludes God but aims to discover universal truths through research, data, and experiments.

**Key methods include:**

- **Empirical Research**
    - Surveys and questionnaires: Gather data on behaviors and attitudes.
    - Experiments: Study cause-and-effect relationships.

- o Observational studies: Observe people's behavior in natural settings.
- o Longitudinal studies: Follow people over time to see how things change.
- **Statistical Analysis**

    - o Descriptive and inferential statistics: Summarize data and make conclusions.
    - o Predictive analytics: Forecast future behaviors based on trends.
- **Theoretical Frameworks**

    - o Various psychological theories like developmental, behavioral, cognitive, and social theories help explain why people behave the way they do.
- **Applied Social Sciences**

    - o **Clinical Psychology and Counseling**: Treat mental health issues.
    - o **Social Work**: Provide resources and support to communities.
    - o **Educational Psychology**: Improve learning and educational methods.

In these approaches, while people are being studied and helped, there's a **big gap**—God isn't invited into the solution.

## Postmodern Social Sciences

Postmodern social sciences go in a different direction. They challenge the idea of universal truths and instead focus on subjective experiences, often trying to deconstruct grand narratives like religion or traditional values.

**Key methods include:**

- **Narrative and Discourse Analysis**

    - o Study personal stories to understand social issues and how language creates power structures.
- **Deconstructive Techniques**

    - o Break down traditional ideas to uncover hidden biases or power dynamics.
- **Critical Theory**

    - o Analyze and challenge societal norms, especially through lenses like race, gender, and sexuality.
- **Participatory Action Research (PAR)**

    - o Engage with communities to co-create solutions to social problems.
- **Visual and Performance Methods**

    - o Use art, photography, and performances to explore and express social issues.

This method often advocates for marginalized groups but operates without a spiritual grounding, leaving out the eternal perspective that faith offers.

## Metamodernism Social Sciences Methodology

Metamodernism is a newer, more fluid way of thinking that swings back and forth between **Modernism** and **Postmodernism**. It tries to combine both perspectives, moving between sincerity and irony, belief and doubt. This methodology reflects that constant **oscillation**—never fully settling in one place.

**Key methods include:**

- **Oscillatory Analysis**

    o Embrace both emotional sincerity and intellectual critique.
    o Combine conviction with doubt, acknowledging both certainty and skepticism.
- **Narrative Integration**

    o Use both grand, universal stories and personal, individual experiences to shape understanding.
- **Cultural Critique**

    o Analyze pop culture, art, and media to understand society's changing beliefs and values.

Metamodernists think it's possible to balance hope and doubt, but as Christians, we know that true hope is grounded in **God's unchanging truth**—not in constantly shifting perspectives.

## Ministry Sciences Methodology

**Ministry Sciences** approach life from a biblical worldview, integrating academic study with spiritual truth. Unlike modernist or postmodernist methodologies, Ministry Sciences invite God into every aspect of care, focusing on transformation through Christ.

**Key methods include:**

- **Biblical Foundation**

    o Root everything in Scripture, where "all Scripture is God-breathed" (2 Timothy 3:16).
- **Prayer**

    o Consistently invite God into the process (1 Thessalonians 5:17).
- **Support a Lifestyle of Love and Moderation**

    o Teach people to love God, love others, and love themselves (Matthew 22:37-39).
- **Ceremonies, Worship, and Small Group Meetings**

- - Create community through gatherings and worship (Hebrews 10:24-25).
- **Academic Investigation**
  - Engage in research that recognizes God's design in creation (Psalm 111:2).
- **Practical Training**
  - Equip Christian leaders through hands-on ministry training (2 Timothy 2:2).
- **Volunteer and Part-Time Ministry**
  - Empower individuals to serve in volunteer or part-time ministry (1 Peter 4:10).
- **Full-Time Ministry and Leadership Development**
  - Offer advanced training and credentialing for full-time ministers (1 Timothy 5:17).
- **Community Building**
  - Foster relationships and peace within the church and community (Romans 14:19).

Ministry Sciences provide a **holistic, hope-filled approach** — grounded in faith — where the ultimate goal is not just to help people cope, but to lead them toward **redemption and wholeness in Christ**.

# Conclusion

In the end, both social sciences and ministry sciences aim to help people, but they come from very different foundations. Modernist, postmodern, and metamodern social sciences focus on research, data, and human solutions — leaving out the spiritual dimension. **Ministry Sciences**, on the other hand, integrate biblical teaching with practical tools, offering real hope through a relationship with God.

As Christians, we have the opportunity to engage with these methodologies and recognize the strengths and limitations of each, all while keeping our eyes fixed on the **eternal truth** that is found in Christ.

**For Further Reading:**

- "Pastoral Care: An Essential Guide" by John Patton
- "Christian Counseling: A Comprehensive Guide" by Gary R. Collins
- "Psychology and Christianity: Five Views" edited by Eric L. Johnson
- "The Healing Path" by Dan Allender
- "Transforming Spirituality: Integrating Theology and Psychology" by F. LeRon Shults and Steven J. Sandage

# The Study of Tropes

## Understanding Tropes and Their Importance: A Christian Perspective

### Introduction: Tropes and Christian Ministry

In **Ministry Sciences**, understanding biblical tropes and their influence on personal and cultural identities is crucial for effective Christian ministry. Tropes—recurring themes, symbols, or motifs—help us communicate complex ideas through familiar frameworks. By exploring these tropes through the lenses of **modernism**, **postmodernism**, **metamodernism**, and **Christian philosophy**, ministry leaders can better connect with individuals in their congregation and help them see how God's truth applies to every aspect of their lives.

Tropes serve as a bridge between stories and real life, reflecting what people believe about their identities, relationships, and purpose. For Christians, these tropes aren't just literary tools—they're deeply tied to **biblical truths** that shape how we live and share the gospel.

## What Are Tropes and Why Do They Matter?

**Tropes** are like shortcuts in storytelling. They are common themes or ideas that we recognize and understand quickly, such as the "hero's journey" or "good vs. evil." Tropes are everywhere—in literature, movies, art, and even in our daily conversations.

For Christians, tropes help us **understand and relate** to biblical teachings in deeper ways. They make spiritual truths more accessible and easier to communicate. By integrating these tropes into sermons, teachings, and personal interactions, Christian leaders can **help people connect with God's story** in a way that resonates with their own experiences.

## Tropes in Christian Ministry: Why They Matter

### 1. Understanding and Relatability

Tropes make complex ideas easier to grasp. For example, when we talk about God as a **shepherd**, people instantly understand His role as a protector and guide. This familiar imagery helps individuals relate to God's care for them on a personal level.

- **Familiar Frameworks:** Using biblical tropes like "God as Father" or "Christ as the Good Shepherd" gives people an immediate sense of the story's meaning. These tropes can help congregations connect their lives to Scripture, making spiritual truths more accessible.

- **Shared Experiences:** When we use tropes that reflect universal human experiences—like love, sacrifice, or redemption—we tap into something that resonates with everyone. For example, the **Prodigal Son** trope speaks to themes of forgiveness and reconciliation, which are relatable to nearly everyone.

## 2. Communication of Values and Lessons

Tropes often carry **moral lessons** that are embedded in Scripture. As Christian ministers, you can use these tropes to communicate the values of the gospel clearly and memorably.

- **Moral Lessons:** Many biblical tropes revolve around virtues like bravery, perseverance, love, and faith. By emphasizing these in your sermons or Bible studies, you provide real-life applications of Christian values. For example, **David vs. Goliath** represents courage in the face of overwhelming odds, teaching believers to trust God in difficult times.

- **Reflection on Life:** Tropes also encourage people to reflect on their own experiences. By relating familiar biblical tropes to everyday struggles or victories, ministers help people see the relevance of God's word in their personal lives.

## 3. Emotional Engagement

Tropes have the power to **engage people emotionally**. When people recognize themselves in a story or resonate with its message, it stirs deep feelings—often leading to spiritual transformation.

- **Eliciting Emotions:** Tropes like **sacrifice** or **forgiveness** tap into universal emotions of love, loss, and redemption. When used effectively, they can help people process their emotions and understand their spiritual journey. The trope of **Christ as the Lamb of God** not only teaches about sacrifice but also evokes gratitude and awe.

- **Comfort and Reassurance:** Tropes such as "God as our Shepherd" or "Jesus calming the storm" offer comfort and assurance during difficult times. These familiar biblical narratives remind us that God is in control and that we are not alone in our struggles.

## 4. Creativity and Imagination

Tropes also encourage **creativity**. While they are familiar, they can be reimagined or presented in new ways to communicate fresh insights into God's word.

- **Sparking Creativity:** For example, a sermon about Jesus as both the **Good Shepherd** and the **Lion of Judah** can bring out the tension and beauty of Christ's character—both gentle and powerful.

- **Expanding Horizons:** Using different biblical and cultural tropes can broaden people's understanding of the world and of faith. For example, exploring how the **early church** lived out the trope of **"community"** (as seen in Acts 2) can inspire modern congregations to embrace a deeper, more authentic Christian fellowship.

## 5. Guidance and Inspiration

Tropes also serve as **role models** for Christian living. They inspire people to follow Christ's example and strive for spiritual growth.

- **Role Models:** Tropes like **Moses leading the Israelites** or **Paul's missionary journeys** serve as examples of leadership, perseverance, and faith. Ministers can point to these biblical characters as guides for facing modern challenges.

- **Aspiration and Motivation:** Tropes motivate people to live out their faith. The image of **Jesus as a Servant** encourages humility, while **Christ as King** inspires believers to pursue God's kingdom with boldness.

## The Role of Tropes in Key Christian Themes

Let's explore how key Christian values are reflected in modern, postmodern, metamodern, and Christian perspectives. These different views shape how people see and understand biblical tropes in culture.

**The Nuclear Family:**

- **Modernist View:** Sees the nuclear family as essential for societal stability.
- **Postmodernist View:** Challenges traditional family models, advocating for more diverse structures.
- **Metamodernist View:** Oscillates between traditional and diverse family models.
- **Christian View:** The family is a sacred institution, designed by God for nurturing faith and fostering discipleship at home.

**Objective Truth and Moral Absolutes:**

- **Modernist View:** Believes in discovering objective truth through science and reason.
- **Postmodernist View:** Argues that truth is relative to culture and perspective.
- **Metamodernist View:** Seeks a balance between universal truth and relative truth.
- **Christian View:** Truth is grounded in God's revelation, and Jesus is the embodiment of ultimate truth.

**Progress and Enlightenment:**

- **Modernist View:** Human progress is achieved through reason and science.
- **Postmodernist View:** Critiques progress, pointing to marginalization and inequality.
- **Metamodernist View:** Both embraces and critiques progress.
- **Christian View:** True progress is spiritual growth, leading toward God's ultimate redemption through Christ.

## How Ministry Sciences Use Tropes

In **Ministry Sciences**, tropes are tools that help communicate deep spiritual truths in an understandable way. As a minister, chaplain, or Christian leader, understanding these tropes can transform your ministry by giving people a clear, relatable framework for their faith. Here are a few foundational Christian tropes and their applications:

- **God as Creator and Designer:** Emphasizing God's role as the creator of all things helps people see purpose in their lives and the world around them.
  **Scripture:** "In the beginning, God created the heavens and the earth." (Genesis 1:1)

- **Every Human is an Image-Bearer:** This powerful truth calls Christians to honor the dignity of every person, promoting justice and equality.
  **Scripture:** "God created man in his own image... male and female he created them." (Genesis 1:27)

- **The Hero of His Story is Jesus the Messiah:** Christ's life, death, and resurrection serve as the ultimate narrative of redemption, and this central trope can be woven into all aspects of Christian teaching.
  **Scripture:** "For there is one God, and one mediator between God and men, the man Christ Jesus." (1 Timothy 2:5)

## Conclusion: Tropes as Stewards of the Christian Faith

Tropes are **powerful tools** that shape how people understand and live out their faith. By understanding these themes, Christian ministers can better communicate the **gospel's relevance** in today's world. When these biblical tropes are embraced, they provide a framework for **meaningful Christian living**, helping people see their own story within God's greater narrative.

Ministers, chaplains, and Christian leaders are **stewards** of these biblical tropes, and by using them wisely, they can guide others toward **spiritual growth, hope, and redemption** in Christ. Whether in preaching, teaching, counseling, or outreach, these familiar and deeply significant themes can **transform lives** and lead people closer to God's purpose for their lives.

## Further Reading List on Tropes and Their Significance

### 1. Theological and Biblical Perspectives on Tropes

- **"Telling the Truth: The Gospel as Tragedy, Comedy, and Fairy Tale"** by Frederick Buechner
  *Publisher:* HarperOne (1997)
  *Summary:* Buechner explores the storytelling elements in the gospel and how biblical narratives mirror the structure of great stories, incorporating tragedy, comedy, and fairy tales. This book highlights the significance of familiar tropes in conveying the gospel message.

- **"Biblical Theology: The God of the Christian Scriptures"** by John Goldingay
  *Publisher:* IVP Academic (2016)
  *Summary:* Goldingay provides a comprehensive view of biblical themes (tropes) and

their theological significance. The book explores how recurring ideas and motifs within the Bible shape Christian doctrine and worldview.

- **"The Drama of Scripture: Finding Our Place in the Biblical Story"** by Craig G. Bartholomew and Michael W. Goheen
  *Publisher:* Baker Academic (2014)
  *Summary:* This book looks at the overarching narrative of the Bible and the recurring themes that define Christian theology. It offers insight into the significance of biblical tropes such as covenant, kingdom, and redemption.

## 2. Tropes in Literature and Storytelling

- **"The Hero with a Thousand Faces"** by Joseph Campbell
  *Publisher:* New World Library (2008)
  *Summary:* Campbell's classic work on myth explores the "hero's journey" as a universal trope in storytelling. This is key to understanding the underlying narrative structures that also appear in biblical and religious stories.

- **"Anatomy of Criticism: Four Essays"** by Northrop Frye
  *Publisher:* Princeton University Press (2000)
  *Summary:* Frye's book delves into the structure of literature, exploring tropes, symbols, and motifs that recur in Western narratives. His insights are useful for analyzing how these elements function in both secular and sacred texts.

- **"Reading Between the Lines: A Christian Guide to Literature"** by Gene Edward Veith Jr.
  *Publisher:* Crossway Books (1990)
  *Summary:* Veith presents a Christian perspective on reading literature, discussing how themes, tropes, and motifs can reveal deeper theological and spiritual truths.

## 3. Tropes in Ministry and Communication

- **"Preaching as Storytelling: Connecting Christian Faith and Narrative"** by David N. Mosser
  *Publisher:* Abingdon Press (2011)
  *Summary:* This book emphasizes the power of using narrative and familiar tropes in preaching. It explores how biblical storytelling can shape sermons and teaching.

- **"The Power of Metaphor: Story Telling & Guideposts for Teaching the Bible"** by Patricia A. McEachern
  *Publisher:* Rowman & Littlefield (2017)
  *Summary:* McEachern discusses how metaphors and tropes can be used in teaching the Bible, offering practical examples of how they enhance understanding and spiritual growth.

- **"Communicating for a Change: Seven Keys to Irresistible Communication"** by Andy Stanley and Lane Jones

*Publisher:* Multnomah (2006)
*Summary:* Stanley explores how effective communicators, especially pastors, can use storytelling and tropes to connect with their audiences and convey biblical truths in relatable ways.

## 4. Tropes and Culture

- **"The Seven Basic Plots: Why We Tell Stories"** by Christopher Booker
  *Publisher:* Bloomsbury Academic (2005)
  *Summary:* Booker explores the seven universal plot tropes that dominate storytelling across cultures. This book is a valuable resource for understanding the tropes that resonate deeply with people and how they apply to biblical stories.

- **"Tropes for the Past: Hayden White and the History/Literature Debate"** edited by Kuisma Korhonen
  *Publisher:* Rodopi (2006)
  *Summary:* This book explores how historical narratives are shaped by literary tropes. It is useful for understanding how historical and religious narratives, including biblical stories, are constructed using familiar thematic patterns.

## 5. Tropes in Philosophy and Christian Thought

- **"Narrative Theology and the Hermeneutical Virtues"** by Jacob L. Goodson
  *Publisher:* Lexington Books (2015)
  *Summary:* Goodson explores how narrative theology incorporates philosophical and literary tropes, offering a way to understand Christian doctrine through story and metaphor.

- **"God in the Dock: Essays on Theology and Ethics"** by C.S. Lewis
  *Publisher:* HarperOne (2014)
  *Summary:* In this collection of essays, Lewis discusses the importance of narrative, myth, and literary tropes in communicating Christian truths. His reflections help readers appreciate how storytelling shapes theology and ethics.

## 6. Tropes in Modern and Postmodern Thought

- **"Truth Decay: Defending Christianity Against the Challenges of Postmodernism"** by Douglas Groothuis
  *Publisher:* IVP Academic (2000)
  *Summary:* Groothuis addresses how postmodern thought affects our understanding of truth and storytelling. The book contrasts secular tropes with biblical narratives, helping Christians reclaim truth in a postmodern world.

- **"Postmodern Times: A Christian Guide to Contemporary Thought and Culture"** by Gene Edward Veith Jr.
  *Publisher:* Crossway Books (1994)

*Summary:* Veith provides insight into how postmodernism impacts culture and philosophy. He offers a Christian critique of postmodern tropes and discusses how these influence contemporary culture and media.

### 7. Tropes in Metamodernism

- **"Metamodernism: The Future of Theory"** by Seth Abramson
  *Publisher:* Springer (2018)
  *Summary:* This work explores metamodernism as a framework that oscillates between modernist and postmodernist ideas, offering a new way to understand cultural tropes in a rapidly changing world.

- **"Notes on Metamodernism"** by Timotheus Vermeulen and Robin van den Akker
  *Publisher:* Platform for Thought in Art and Culture (2010)
  *Summary:* This text introduces metamodernism, discussing its role in reshaping cultural and philosophical narratives. It explores how metamodern tropes reflect a balance of sincerity and irony, which can influence religious and social thought.

# The Study of Muliplying Christian Leaders

### Multiplying Christian Leaders of the Ministry Sciences Movement

At the core of the **Ministry Sciences** movement is a powerful question: *How do Christian leaders multiply their influence while living out their calling?* This chapter explores how effective leadership in ministry isn't just about knowing the right things but embodying the principles of faith in everyday life. These leaders aren't just instructors—they're role models, visionaries, and mentors who spread their faith to others. Through their actions and example, they empower others to become agents of God's redemption.

### Visionaries of Change

The leaders of the Ministry Sciences movement are more than teachers—they're **visionaries** who see the potential in every Christian to be a **conduit of God's grace**. They don't just share knowledge but ignite transformation, helping people walk with God and, in turn, share that faith with others. This vision ties together spiritual growth with real-world ministry, grounded in both **biblical teachings** and addressing the challenges of modern life.

### The Organic Methodology of Ministry Sciences

A key element of Ministry Sciences is its **organic approach** to leadership. Ministry is about spiritual growth, but also about spreading the Gospel like seeds sown by a farmer. Jesus explained this idea in the **Parable of the Sower** (Matthew 13:3-8), showing how Christian leaders are like farmers sowing seeds. Some seeds will fall on hard soil, but others will take root, grow, and multiply—some even one hundred times!

Ministry Sciences focuses on this *organic multiplication*—where leaders go out, share the Word of God, and see lives transformed through the power of the Holy Spirit. Christian leadership isn't about forcing results but planting seeds and trusting God to bring growth. Leaders are like sowers who spread the Gospel, confident that **God's Word** will never return empty but will accomplish what He intends (Isaiah 55:11).

## Christian Leaders Who Multiply

In Ministry Sciences, Christian leaders are seen as more than teachers—they are multipliers. The **Christian Leaders Institute** helps these leaders understand how to share their faith and multiply it in others. There are **seven key connections** for multiplying Christian leaders:

1. **Personal Connection**: Every leader must first be transformed by their personal relationship with God, rooted in daily prayer, Bible reading, and communion with the Holy Spirit.
2. **Marital Connection**: For those who are married, faith is deeply intertwined with their spouse, and marriage becomes a way to grow in faith together.
3. **Family Connection**: For parents, sharing faith with their children is vital. This can include everything from family prayers to Christian homeschooling.
4. **Small Group Connection**: Small groups offer a place for Christians to study the Bible and grow in their faith together, deepening their walk with God.
5. **Church and Worship Connection**: Church services and sermons help Christians share their faith, and Ministry Sciences trains leaders to preach and lead churches effectively.
6. **Kingdom Connection**: This connects Christians to a global movement, linking local churches with Christian schools, ministries, and organizations.
7. **Evangelistic Connection**: Ultimately, all Christians are called to spread the Gospel to those who don't know God. Leaders are trained to reach out and share their testimonies.

## Diverse Leadership Roles

The Ministry Sciences movement recognizes a variety of roles within Christian leadership:

- **Officiants**: These leaders perform weddings, funerals, and other significant ceremonies, guiding people through important life events with faith.
- **Licensed and Ordained Ministers**: Ministers who preach, teach, and lead churches.
- **Coaching Ministers**: These leaders guide others in personal growth and spiritual development.
- **Ministry Chaplains**: Chaplains bring ministry into hospitals, the military, and other non-church settings, providing care in challenging environments.

## The Power of Testimonies

In Christianity, **testimonies** are powerful stories of personal encounters with God. They show

how lives have been transformed by faith. These stories are shared to encourage others and provide hope that God can work in anyone's life. The Bible itself is full of testimonies, from the apostles who witnessed Jesus' resurrection to modern-day Christians who share how God has changed their lives.

Testimonies in the Ministry Sciences movement are not just personal—they are methodologically sound. Just as scientific methods use evidence, testimonies provide living evidence of God's power at work. These stories connect faith with practical life and encourage others to seek transformation through Jesus Christ.

## Training Christian Leaders

Jesus' ministry was about **training leaders** who would carry on His work. He taught His disciples through **Scripture** and practical experience, like when He sent them out to preach and heal (Luke 10). Ministry Sciences builds on this model, training Christian leaders to study Scripture, preach the Gospel, and lead others.

In the New Testament, leaders like the Apostle Paul and Timothy were encouraged to study God's Word and share it with others (2 Timothy 2:15). This passion for studying and sharing Scripture is central to Ministry Sciences, equipping leaders to be effective in their calling.

## Christian Leaders in Action

The ultimate goal of Ministry Sciences is to **equip Christian leaders** to make a real difference in their communities. These leaders go out into the world, sharing the **Gospel** and multiplying their faith in others. Whether they are officiating a wedding, leading a Bible study, or providing spiritual care as chaplains, they embody the transformative power of faith.

Christian leaders, empowered by the Holy Spirit, are the key to spreading Christianity. Their personal experiences and testimonies become a living example of God's work. As Jesus said, His followers would do even greater things than He did (John 14:12)—and this happens when leaders multiply their faith in others.

## Conclusion

Ministry Sciences is about more than just learning—it's about living out your faith in a way that transforms others. Christian leaders are not only equipped with knowledge but are empowered by the Holy Spirit to make a difference. As they share their testimonies and walk with God, they fulfill the Great Commission to make disciples of all nations (Matthew 28:19). These leaders are the **multipliers** of Christianity, spreading their influence far beyond themselves and continuing the work that Jesus started.

**For Further Reading:**

- **"The Master Plan of Evangelism"** by Robert E. Coleman
  Publisher: Revell

*A guide to multiplying Christian leaders through discipleship.*

- **"Spiritual Leadership: Principles of Excellence for Every Believer"** by J. Oswald Sanders
  Publisher: Moody Publishers
  *Practical insights for Christian leaders on how to develop their leadership skills and influence others.*
- **"Multiply: Disciples Making Disciples"** by Francis Chan
  Publisher: David C. Cook
  *Guidance on making disciples who will make more disciples, multiplying the movement of Christian leadership.*

# The Study of Reproducible Connections

## Reproducible Connections for Multiplying Christian Leaders

**Introduction**

With over two billion Christians worldwide, the call to spread and multiply our faith is a massive and global mission. At **Christian Leaders Institute**, we emphasize the importance of seven key connections that help Christians multiply their faith effectively. These connections are at the heart of **Ministry Sciences** and serve as a framework for Christian leaders, whether they are active Christians, volunteer, part-time, or full-time officiants and ministers. Each connection plays a vital role in the mission to spread the Gospel and create more disciples.

A special acknowledgment goes to Steve Elzinga, a ministry partner and longtime friend, who developed this **seven-connection approach** as a way to create reproducible Christianity. First introduced in the 1990s, this approach has since been taught at Christian Leaders Institute and through the **Christian Leaders Alliance**. Today, we continue to see its powerful impact as it trains Christian leaders in effective ministry.

### 1. Personal Connection

**Concept**

The **Personal Connection** is the foundation of a Christian leader's life. It refers to a deep, transformative relationship with God through daily prayer, Bible reading, and communion with the Holy Spirit. This connection not only helps individuals grow spiritually but also sets an example for others to follow.

**Biblical Foundation**

- *Prayer*: "Rejoice always. Pray without ceasing. In everything give thanks, for this is the

will of God in Christ Jesus toward you" (1 Thessalonians 5:16-18, WEB).
- *Bible Reading*: "Your word is a lamp to my feet, and a light for my path" (Psalm 119:105, WEB).
- *Communion with the Holy Spirit*: "But the Counselor, the Holy Spirit, whom the Father will send in my name, he will teach you all things, and will remind you of all that I said to you" (John 14:26, WEB).

**Reproduction Strategy**

- **Model Personal Devotion**: Demonstrate a consistent, authentic walk with God. Share personal stories of how daily prayer and Bible study have transformed your life.
- **Mentorship**: Encourage and mentor others in building their own relationship with God. Use Bible study plans, prayer guides, and regular check-ins to help them grow spiritually.
- **Training**: Offer workshops and seminars on spiritual disciplines like Bible study and prayer. Provide practical tools for others to deepen their personal connection with God.

**Conclusion**

The Personal Connection is crucial for spiritual growth and sets the stage for multiplying faith in others. By mentoring others, modeling devotion, and providing training, Christian leaders can help others cultivate a deep, lasting relationship with God.

## 2. Marital Connection

### Concept

For those who are married, the **Marital Connection** plays a key role in their spiritual journey. A Christ-centered marriage involves praying together, studying the Bible together, and inviting God into the relationship.

### Biblical Foundation

- *Shared Prayer*: "Again, assuredly I tell you, that if two of you will agree on earth concerning anything that they will ask, it will be done for them by my Father who is in heaven" (Matthew 18:19, WEB).
- *Bible Study Together*: "Let the word of Christ dwell in you richly; in all wisdom teaching and admonishing one another with psalms, hymns, and spiritual songs" (Colossians 3:16, WEB).
- *God in the Relationship*: "A cord of three strands is not quickly broken" (Ecclesiastes 4:12, WEB).

**Reproduction Strategy**

- **Romance and Marriage Ministry**: Encourage officiants to create ministries that focus on dating, engagement, and marriage. Offer marriage enrichment programs and pre-marriage counseling that emphasize spiritual growth.
- **Couple's Ministry**: Host retreats, Bible studies, and prayer sessions for couples. Equip them with tools for growing spiritually as a couple.
- **Counseling and Support**: Offer marital counseling rooted in biblical principles.

Establish support groups where couples can seek advice and encouragement from others.

**Conclusion**

A Christ-centered marriage is not only fulfilling but also provides a strong testimony to others. By focusing on marital connection, Christian leaders help couples grow spiritually and create lasting, God-centered relationships.

## 3. Family Connection

**Concept**

Families are essential for passing down the Christian faith to future generations. Teaching children about God and modeling a Christian life can leave a lasting legacy of faith.

**Biblical Foundation**

- *Teaching Children*: "Train up a child in the way he should go, and when he is old he will not depart from it" (Proverbs 22:6, WEB).
- *Modeling a Christian Life*: "You shall teach them diligently to your children, and talk of them when you sit in your house, when you walk by the way, when you lie down, and when you rise up" (Deuteronomy 6:7, WEB).

**Reproduction Strategy**

- **Family Devotions**: Encourage families to have regular Bible study and prayer times. Provide resources like devotionals and family prayer guides.
- **Christian Education**: Support the development of Christian homeschooling, academies, and mentoring programs that integrate faith with learning.
- **Parental Training**: Offer workshops that help parents teach and model the Christian faith to their children effectively.

**Conclusion**

By fostering strong family connections, Christian leaders can help ensure that the faith is passed down through generations, creating a ripple effect of spiritual growth and leadership.

## 4. Small Group Connection

**Concept**

Small groups are a vital way for Christians to grow in their faith, build relationships, and study the Word of God together.

**Biblical Foundation**

- *Supportive Environment*: "Let us consider how to provoke one another to love and good works" (Hebrews 10:24-25, WEB).

- *Studying the Word*: "All Scripture is inspired by God and is profitable for teaching" (2 Timothy 3:16, WEB).

**Reproduction Strategy**

- **Group Formation**: Create small groups within the church that focus on Bible study, prayer, and accountability.
- **Leadership Development**: Train small group leaders to effectively guide others in their spiritual journey.
- **Resources**: Provide study materials and discussion guides to keep groups focused and productive.

**Conclusion**

Small groups are an essential way to foster spiritual growth and create meaningful relationships. Christian leaders can multiply their influence by forming and equipping small groups to spread the Gospel.

## 5. Church and Worship Connection

**Concept**

Church services and communal worship are central to Christian life. They provide a space for hearing God's Word, worshiping together, and experiencing spiritual nourishment.

**Biblical Foundation**

- *Hearing the Word*: "Faith comes by hearing, and hearing by the word of God" (Romans 10:17, WEB).
- *Worship Together*: "Let us make a joyful noise to the rock of our salvation!" (Psalm 95:1, WEB).

**Reproduction Strategy**

- **Preaching Training**: Equip pastors and leaders with the skills needed to preach and teach effectively.
- **Worship Leadership**: Train worship leaders to create meaningful, God-centered worship experiences.
- **Community Engagement**: Encourage churches to engage with their local communities through outreach programs and services.

**Conclusion**

Churches and worship services are the heart of Christian community life. By training leaders and fostering vibrant worship experiences, Christian leaders can multiply their reach and influence.

## 6. Kingdom Connection

## Concept

The **Kingdom Connection** links local churches and Christians to the global Christian community, uniting them in the mission to spread the Gospel worldwide.

## Biblical Foundation

- *Global Christian Community*: "There is one body, and one Spirit" (Ephesians 4:4, WEB).
- *Spreading the Gospel*: "Go into all the world, and preach the Good News" (Mark 16:15, WEB).

## Reproduction Strategy

- **Soul and Mentor Centers**: Establish centers where Christians can gather for worship, study, and leadership development.
- **Global Partnerships**: Build partnerships with international Christian organizations and missions.
- **Education and Training**: Support Christian schools and academies that equip future Christian leaders.

## Conclusion

The Kingdom Connection unites Christians globally in the mission to spread the Gospel. By fostering partnerships and supporting Christian education, Christian leaders can build a network of disciples dedicated to advancing God's kingdom.

# 7. Evangelistic Connection

## Concept

The **Evangelistic Connection** is the final goal of the other six connections—reaching non-Christians and sharing the Gospel.

## Biblical Foundation

- *Great Commission*: "Go and make disciples of all nations" (Matthew 28:19-20, WEB).
- *Sharing the Gospel*: "You will be witnesses to me in Jerusalem, in all Judea and Samaria, and to the uttermost parts of the earth" (Acts 1:8, WEB).

## Reproduction Strategy

- **Evangelism Training**: Provide training that equips Christians to confidently and compassionately share their faith.
- **Outreach Programs**: Develop outreach initiatives that address community needs while providing opportunities to share the Gospel.
- **Testimony Sharing**: Encourage believers to share their testimonies as a powerful tool for evangelism.

## Conclusion

The evangelistic connection brings the mission full circle by training Christians to spread the Gospel to non-believers. Through effective evangelism strategies, Christian leaders can inspire others to come to faith and multiply the Christian community.

**Summary**

By focusing on these seven key connections—Personal, Marital, Family, Small Group, Church and Worship, Kingdom, and Evangelistic—Christian leaders can effectively multiply their faith and create lasting, transformative impact. These reproducible connections are the cornerstone of the Ministry Sciences approach, ensuring the continued growth and spreading of Christianity.

**For Further Reading:**

1   **"The Secret to a Great Music Ministry" by Steven Elzinga**
    *Publisher:* Bible League
    *Publication Date:* 2003
    *Comments:* This book offers practical steps for building a thriving music ministry, focusing on engaging attendees and integrating music as a key part of spiritual life.

2   **"The Secret to a Great Preaching Ministry" by Steven Elzinga**
    *Publisher:* Bible League
    *Publication Date:* 2003
    *Comments:* Elzinga shares insights into impactful preaching, emphasizing not just delivery but preparing listeners' hearts to receive the message.

3   **"The Secret to a Great Evangelism Ministry" by Steven Elzinga**
    *Publisher:* Bible League
    *Publication Date:* 2003
    *Comments:* This book focuses on cultivating a personal walk with God that naturally fuels enthusiasm for sharing the Gospel with others.

4   **"Christian Leaders Life Coach Minister" by Steve Elzinga**
    *Publisher:* Christian Leaders Institute
    *Publication Date:* 2019
    *Comments:* A comprehensive guide for those pursuing life coaching ministry, combining biblical principles with practical advice for coaching others.

5   **"Genesis: The Foundation of Everything" by Steve Elzinga**
    *Publisher:* Christian Leaders Institute
    *Comments:* This Bible study delves into the book of Genesis, exploring its key themes and their relevance to the rest of the Bible. It's ideal for small groups or sermon series, offering a foundational understanding of God's plan for humanity.

6   **"Acts: The Unbelievable Story of the Church" by Steve Elzinga**
    *Publisher:* Christian Leaders Institute

*Comments:* A study of the book of Acts that highlights the growth of the early church and the spread of the Gospel, inspiring modern believers to live boldly like the early Christians.

7 **"Ephesians: Who are You?" by Steve Elzinga**
*Publisher:* Christian Leaders Institute
*Comments:* This Bible study focuses on identity in Christ and practical applications for living out faith, making it a suitable resource for personal study, small groups, or sermon series.

8 **"The Jesus Bible" by Steve Elzinga**
*Publisher:* Christian Leaders Institute
*Publication Date:* 2017
*Comments:* A resource that organizes biblical content about Jesus into accessible categories, making it a useful tool for study and teaching.

9 **"The Sampler Bible" by Steve Elzinga**
*Publisher:* Christian Leaders Institute
*Publication Date:* 2019
*Comments:* A curated collection of Bible passages with helpful notes, designed to support personal study and ministry efforts.

10 **"Being a Lifeboat Church in a Cruise Ship World" by Steven Elzinga**
*Publisher:* Pathway Ministries
*Publication Date:* 2012
*Comments:* Using the Titanic as a metaphor, this book explores how churches can avoid becoming inward-focused and instead prioritize outreach and evangelism.

# The Study of Ministry

## The Cultural Brand of Minister: The Role of Diakonos – A Servant Leadership Revolution

## What is Cultural Branding?

Cultural branding happens when a specific concept, word, or role becomes a part of a community's identity and values. It shapes how people in that culture see and understand those terms. For example, some words might take on new meanings and expectations, based on how they're used and understood by that group.

## Ministers in History: A Shift in Meaning

Imagine you're in the Netherlands around 1900. The minister at your church is called the "Domini," a word from Latin that means "Lord." In this church, the minister is a highly respected leader, almost seen as a ruler. Jump ahead to the 1960s or 70s, and Dutch immigrants in a church are now calling the minister "Dominy" as a friendly nickname. But even though the name is warmer, it still carries an idea of authority.

But this isn't how ministry started in the early church. The word "minister" actually comes from the Latin word *ministrae* and the Greek word *diakonos,* which means "servant." This understanding of leadership—where the leader is a servant—is how early Christians saw their leaders. This was a huge shift from how most cultures viewed leadership, and it changed the way Christians thought about what it meant to be a leader.

## The Word *Diakonos* and Ministry

In the New Testament, the Greek word *diakonos* is used to describe someone who serves others. This word is sometimes translated as "servant," "deacon," or "minister." Whenever you see it in the Bible, it's important to remember that it's about serving people. Early church leaders were known as "servant ministers," showing how they viewed leadership as an act of service.

## Examples of *Diakonos* in the Bible

Let's look at some Bible verses where *diakonos* is used. These passages give us a clear picture of how the early church viewed leadership.

- **Matthew 20:26 (WEB):** "It shall not be so among you, but whoever desires to become great among you shall be your servant (diakonos)."

    o   Jesus explains that true greatness in God's kingdom comes from serving others.
- **John 2:5, 9 (WEB):** "His mother said to the servants (diakonos), 'Whatever he says to you, do it.'"

    o   At the wedding in Cana, the servants play a key role in Jesus's first miracle. They show that being ready to serve is important.
- **Romans 16:1 (WEB):** "I commend to you our sister Phoebe, a minister (diakonos) of the church at Cenchreae."

    o   Phoebe, a woman leader, is called a *diakonos*, showing that both men and women

were seen as servant leaders in the early church.
These examples show that Jesus and the apostles taught that leaders should serve, not dominate. Christian leadership is about humility, faithfulness, and helping others grow in faith.

## What We Learn About Christian Leadership from *Diakonos*

When we study the word *diakonos* in the New Testament, a few key ideas stand out:

1 **Servanthood:** Christian leaders are called to serve others, not to control or dominate them. Jesus modeled this kind of leadership.

2 **Humility:** Greatness in God's kingdom is measured by how well we serve others.

3 **Faithfulness and Integrity:** A good Christian leader is trustworthy, faithful, and committed to doing what's right.

4 **Inclusivity:** Both men and women can be called to serve as leaders. The early church was open to different kinds of people stepping into these roles.

5 **Teaching and Care:** Christian leaders help others grow by teaching them and caring for their needs.

## Christian Leaders Alliance: Serving Like *Diakonos*

The Christian Leaders Alliance (CLA) takes this idea of *diakonos* seriously. They believe all Christian leaders, whether they're officiants, ministers, or chaplains, should serve others with humility and compassion.

- **Officiants:** These are leaders who help with ceremonies like weddings, baptisms, and funerals. They serve people at the most important moments of their lives.

- **Licensed and Ordained Ministers:** These leaders take care of congregations, teaching, preaching, and providing care. They model servant leadership by putting others' needs first.

- **Coaching Ministers:** Coaching ministers help people grow in their faith. They focus on helping others reach their potential in Christ, showing that leading is about serving.

- **Chaplain Ministers:** These leaders serve people in tough places like hospitals, prisons, and the military. They bring comfort and hope to those who are struggling.

## Conclusion

The word *diakonos* teaches us that Christian leadership is all about service. Jesus flipped the idea of leadership on its head when He said, "If you want to be great, be a servant." Christian leaders today can look to the early church's example of leadership that is humble, inclusive, and faithful. This kind of leadership can transform churches and communities, showing the world that real power lies in serving others.

## For Further Reading:

- "The Jesus Way: A Conversation on the Ways That Jesus Is the Way" by Eugene H. Peterson
  **Publisher:** Eerdmans
  **Date:** 2007
  Peterson explores how Jesus led as a servant and what that means for leadership today.

- "Building a StoryBrand: Clarify Your Message So Customers Will Listen" by Donald Miller
  **Publisher:** HarperCollins Leadership
  **Date:** 2017
  Miller helps leaders communicate clearly by focusing on how they can serve others.

- "The Servant: A Simple Story About the True Essence of Leadership" by James C. Hunter
  **Publisher:** Crown Business
  **Date:** 1998
  This book explains how being a servant leader can make a big difference in both life and ministry.

# The Study of Roles and Credentialling

In **Ministry Sciences**, the study of ministry roles is grounded in both biblical and contemporary practice. The ancient roles of **prophets, priests**, and **ministers** in the Bible—central to the spiritual life and leadership of Israel and the early church—have their echoes in today's diverse ministry roles. Four prominent modern roles that carry forward these biblical responsibilities are **Officiant, Minister, Coaching Minister**, and **Chaplain**. Each of these roles fulfills a specific function within the church and society, reflecting elements of the prophetic, priestly, and ministerial functions seen throughout biblical history.

This chapter explores how these modern ministry roles serve as **contemporary examples** of biblical leadership, grounding their authority and practice in the ancient traditions of **prophets, priests**, and **ministers**.

### The Officiant: A Modern Reflection of the Priest

**1. Role Overview** The **Officiant** serves a unique function in both sacred and public ceremonies, primarily officiating rites such as **weddings, funerals, baptisms**, and other important life events. Much like the biblical priests, officiants today act as intermediaries between God and people, sanctifying moments that bring communities together and recognizing sacred milestones in life.

In biblical times, **priests** were responsible for facilitating **sacrificial worship**, **maintaining the temple**, and **interceding** on behalf of the people. The role of today's officiant, while adapted for modern times, still carries a sacred trust to guide individuals through significant life events while invoking God's blessing and presence.

**2. Key Responsibilities**

- **Sanctifying Sacred Events**: Officiants conduct ceremonies that bring people into an awareness of the sacred. Whether it's the joyful union of a couple in marriage or a solemn funeral, the officiant helps people recognize and respond to God's work in their lives.

- **Teaching and Guiding**: Similar to the **priests** of the Bible who taught the Law to the people, officiants often guide couples through pre-marital counseling or provide spiritual comfort to grieving families before and after ceremonies.

- **Interceding for Others**: Like the priests who interceded for Israel through sacrifice, the officiant prays on behalf of those participating in the ceremony, whether asking for God's blessing on a marriage, grace for the deceased, or sanctification in a baptism.

**3. Credentialing and Ministry Sciences Application** Officiants in modern contexts are typically credentialed through **ordination** or **licensing**, enabling them to legally and spiritually conduct these rites. This practice echoes the consecration of priests in the Bible, who were set apart through ritual acts to serve God's people. In **Ministry Sciences**, the officiant is trained to understand the theological significance of ceremonies, combining biblical knowledge with the ability to facilitate profound, meaningful spiritual experiences.

## The Minister: A Contemporary Prophet and Shepherd

**1. Role Overview** The **Minister** encompasses both the **prophetic** and **shepherding** aspects of biblical leadership. Ministers are often called to **preach**, **teach**, and provide **spiritual oversight** to communities, much like the prophets of old who declared God's word, and the priests who guided people in their spiritual walk.

In biblical times, **prophets** were God's mouthpieces, delivering His messages and calling for repentance, while **priests** maintained the covenant community through worship and instruction. Ministers today function as a combination of both these roles—proclaiming biblical truths while shepherding people through their spiritual journeys.

**2. Key Responsibilities**

- **Proclaiming God's Word**: Ministers act as modern-day prophets by preaching the gospel and teaching biblical truths. Like the prophet **Isaiah** or **Jeremiah**, ministers challenge, encourage, and guide people toward living in alignment with God's will.

- **Shepherding the Flock**: Ministers, in their pastoral role, reflect the **priestly** function of caring for the spiritual well-being of their communities. They provide counseling, support during crises, and discipleship to help people grow in their faith.

- **Equipping the Saints**: Ministers also train and equip their congregations to serve others. In the New Testament, the Apostle Paul wrote that ministers are called to "equip the saints for the work of ministry, for building up the body of Christ" (Ephesians 4:12, WEB).

**3. Credentialing and Ministry Sciences Application** Ministers are often **ordained** after undergoing formal theological education and practical ministry training. In **Ministry Sciences**, ministers are seen as vital leaders who bridge the gap between the prophetic call of proclaiming God's truth and the pastoral care necessary for nurturing spiritual growth. This role is critical in guiding people to both personal transformation and active service in the church.

## The Coaching Minister: The Encourager and Discipler

**1. Role Overview** The **Coaching Minister** is a relatively new but growing role that incorporates the principles of **life coaching** into ministry. Coaching Ministers, like the **prophets** and **priests** of the Bible, help individuals discern their **calling**, overcome **obstacles**, and align their lives with God's purpose. They serve as **mentors** and **guides**, helping people identify where God is at work in their lives and how to live out their faith in practical ways.

The biblical **priests** and **prophets** often acted as coaches, providing spiritual counsel to kings, leaders, and the people of Israel. Moses, for example, provided **leadership coaching** to Joshua (Numbers 27:18-23), preparing him for his future role as the leader of Israel.

**2. Key Responsibilities**

- **Guiding Personal Growth**: Coaching ministers help individuals set spiritual and personal goals, much like the biblical prophets who called people back to their covenantal commitments. Coaching ministers encourage spiritual growth, personal development, and godly decision-making.

- **Offering Accountability**: Just as **Elijah** mentored **Elisha** and held him accountable in his spiritual growth, coaching ministers provide accountability in their discipleship relationships, ensuring people stay on track in their walk with God.

- **Fostering Transformation**: Coaching ministers focus on **transformational discipleship**, using coaching principles to encourage life change. In many ways, this echoes the role of **Samuel** as he guided the nation of Israel through leadership transitions, calling for spiritual renewal and alignment with God's will.

**3. Credentialing and Ministry Sciences Application** Coaching ministers often undergo **life**

**coaching** certification alongside their theological training. In **Ministry Sciences**, coaching ministers are seen as key players in facilitating personal and spiritual transformation. Their role complements traditional pastoral care by focusing on individual growth and empowering believers to take responsibility for their spiritual journey.

## The Chaplain: A Contemporary Shepherd and Intercessor

**1. Role Overview** The **Chaplain** serves in diverse environments, including **hospitals**, **military bases**, **corporate settings**, and even **online**. Chaplains function much like the biblical **priests** who served in sacred spaces and the **prophets** who interceded for others. Their ministry is one of **presence**, **comfort**, and **spiritual guidance**, offering care in times of crisis and transition.

Chaplains in the Bible, like **Aaron** and the Levites, were tasked with maintaining the spiritual health of the nation, offering sacrifices, and ensuring the people's connection to God. Today's chaplains provide **pastoral care** in various settings, often outside the traditional church context.

**2. Key Responsibilities**

- **Providing Spiritual Care**: Chaplains offer spiritual support to individuals in crisis, such as patients in hospitals, soldiers in the military, or employees in workplaces. They pray for and with people, provide counseling, and offer comfort during difficult times.

- **Interceding in Crisis**: Much like **Moses** interceded for the Israelites, chaplains serve as spiritual intercessors in critical moments. They pray for those in their care, helping them navigate spiritual, emotional, and ethical challenges.

- **Bridging Secular and Sacred**: Chaplains often minister in secular environments, acting as bridges between **faith** and **everyday life**. They provide spiritual wisdom in spaces where traditional church roles may not reach.

**3. Credentialing and Ministry Sciences Application** Chaplains typically undergo **specialized training** in chaplaincy, along with theological education. In **Ministry Sciences**, chaplains are seen as essential extensions of pastoral care, bringing God's presence into places that might otherwise be disconnected from traditional church ministry. Their work highlights the importance of ministry in all areas of life, not just within the church walls.

## Conclusion: Officiant, Minister, Coaching Minister, and Chaplain as Prophets, Priests, and Ministers Today

The modern roles of **Officiant**, **Minister**, **Coaching Minister**, and **Chaplain** serve as **contemporary reflections** of the **prophets**, **priests**, and **ministers** of the biblical era. These roles demonstrate the enduring need for spiritual leadership, guidance, and care across various aspects of life. In **Ministry Sciences**, these roles are seen not just as functional positions, but as **vocations** that carry forward the rich tradition of biblical leadership, adapted to meet the needs of today's world.

Through these roles, the church continues to embody the **prophetic**, **priestly**, and **ministerial** callings seen in Scripture, while embracing the evolving needs of contemporary society. Whether officiating a wedding, leading a congregation, coaching individuals in their faith journey, or offering comfort in a hospital room, these modern ministers continue the work of **proclaiming**, **serving**, and **interceding**—just as the prophets, priests, and ministers of the Bible did centuries ago.

## Volunteer, Part-Time, and Career Track Ministry Roles: Flexibility in Service and the Importance of Affordable Training

In **Ministry Sciences**, the roles of **Officiant**, **Minister**, **Coaching Minister**, and **Chaplain** can be tailored to fit different levels of engagement. Individuals may serve as **volunteers**, take on **part-time roles**, or commit to **full-time ministry careers**, depending on their personal calling and life circumstances. This flexibility ensures that people can serve in ministry while balancing other responsibilities. However, a key challenge for many individuals entering ministry— especially for **volunteers** and **part-time ministers**—is the **cost of training and education**.

To address this challenge, **donation-supported ministry training schools** play an essential role by providing affordable and often **debt-free** educational opportunities. These schools allow individuals to **answer their call to ministry** without the financial burden of student loans. Additionally, **low-cost credentialing programs** help those who pursue **full-time ministry careers** stay out of debt and prepare for their roles, as salaries in ministry are often lower than in other fields.

## Ministry Roles Across Different Tracks

### 1. Volunteer Track

The **volunteer track** is perfect for individuals who want to serve but cannot commit to ministry as a full-time career. Volunteers are often essential to **small churches**, **community ministries**, and **online faith communities**, where paid staff may be limited.

- **Officiant (Volunteer)**: Volunteer officiants may perform **weddings**, **baptisms**, and **funerals** for friends, family, and local communities. Since their ministry is often limited to specific events, their training can be less extensive. **Donation-supported training schools** help make this training accessible, allowing volunteers to gain the credentials they need without accumulating debt.

- **Minister (Volunteer)**: Volunteer ministers serve in smaller settings, leading **Bible studies**, **offering pastoral care**, or assisting with church services. These roles are vital in **house churches**, **small congregations**, and **mission fields**. Because these ministers often do not receive compensation, it's crucial that their education is affordable. Ministry training schools that rely on **donations** provide the resources for these volunteers to gain **basic ministry credentials**, ensuring they are well-equipped for their roles without the financial strain of traditional education.

- **Coaching Minister (Volunteer)**: Volunteer coaching ministers help guide others through **life's challenges** and **spiritual growth**. These roles may be informal and focus on **mentorship** or **one-on-one counseling**. Volunteer coaching ministers benefit from **low-cost or free certification programs** that prepare them to serve effectively without the financial burden of more extensive, professional coaching training.

- **Chaplain (Volunteer)**: Volunteer chaplains work in places like **hospitals**, **disaster relief efforts**, and **corporate environments**, providing **spiritual care** during times of need. The cost of chaplaincy training can be high, but donation-supported schools allow volunteer chaplains to access the training they need without incurring debt, enabling them to offer essential services to their communities.

**Study Requirement for Volunteers**: Volunteer roles typically require **short-term training programs** that focus on **practical ministry skills**. **Donation-supported training** and **scholarship opportunities** are essential to keep education accessible, ensuring volunteers can serve without the weight of financial obligations. This model enables churches and ministries to grow without needing to rely solely on paid staff.

## 2. Part-Time Track

The **part-time track** is for individuals who wish to commit more time to ministry but also need to balance another job or vocation. Part-time ministers might work in **bi-vocational roles**, combining ministry with secular employment. For these ministers, affordable training and credentialing options are key to enabling them to pursue their calling while managing other responsibilities.

- **Officiant (Part-Time)**: Part-time officiants may perform **multiple ceremonies** throughout the year and provide **ongoing pastoral support** to families. Their work may also include **premarital counseling** or **baptism classes**. Since officiants often balance this role with other employment, low-cost ministry training schools are essential to ensure that they can receive proper credentials without financial hardship.

- **Minister (Part-Time)**: Part-time ministers serve in **small churches**, **church plants**, or **mission settings** where full-time clergy may not be needed. These ministers often lead **worship**, **preach**, and provide **pastoral care**. Training for part-time ministers typically involves **seminary coursework** or **theological studies**, and affordable credentialing programs enable them to gain the necessary skills without jeopardizing their financial well-being. Since part-time ministers often have limited income from ministry work, access to **donation-supported schools** is crucial.

- **Coaching Minister (Part-Time)**: Part-time coaching ministers guide people through **spiritual formation, personal development**, and **life transitions**. Many coach in churches or **community centers**, helping individuals discover their gifts and calling. The availability of **low-cost training programs** and **certification courses** allows part-time coaches to get the education they need without large financial commitments, making it possible for them to balance ministry with other jobs.

- **Chaplain (Part-Time)**: Part-time chaplains may work in **healthcare**, **corporate**, or **military settings**, providing **spiritual care** during their shifts or on an as-needed basis. Training for part-time chaplains often includes **chaplaincy certification** and **clinical pastoral education (CPE)**. However, full CPE programs can be expensive, so **donation-supported schools** are essential for part-time chaplains who want to enter the field without taking on significant debt.

**Study Requirement for Part-Time Ministers**: Part-time ministry roles typically require **moderate training**, including **certification programs** and **seminary courses**. These programs must be **affordable** to accommodate individuals who work in both secular and ministry roles. The ability to access **scholarship-supported education** ensures that part-time ministers can serve without incurring heavy financial burdens.

## 3. Career Track

The **career track** is for individuals who feel called to pursue **full-time ministry** as their life's work. These roles require significant **theological training** and **professional development**, as career ministers are responsible for **leading congregations**, **planting churches**, or overseeing **chaplaincy programs**. However, many full-time ministers face lower salaries, so **low-cost credentialing** is crucial for helping them pursue their calling without the pressure of large student loan payments.

- **Officiant (Career Track)**: Career officiants often work full-time within **churches** or **ministry organizations**, performing numerous ceremonies throughout the year and providing ongoing pastoral care. Full-time officiants may teach **marriage preparation classes** or lead **baptism ministries**. They typically require **seminary education** or extensive **pastoral training**, and **donation-supported ministry schools** provide an affordable path to gain these credentials without incurring significant debt.

- **Minister (Career Track)**: Full-time ministers serve as **senior pastors**, **associate pastors**, or **executive ministers** in large congregations or ministry organizations. They are responsible for **preaching**, **discipleship**, **strategic planning**, and **pastoral care**. Career ministers often pursue a **Master of Divinity (MDiv)** or other advanced theological degrees, but these degrees can be expensive. **Low-cost ministry schools** supported by donations enable full-time ministers to get the education they need without being overwhelmed by debt, especially considering that salaries in full-time ministry are often modest.

- **Coaching Minister (Career Track)**: Full-time coaching ministers may lead **spiritual coaching ministries**, developing **life coaching programs** and helping individuals or groups in the church grow spiritually and personally. Career coaching ministers often require both **theological education** and **professional coaching certification**, but affordable training options are vital. **Donation-supported training programs** and **scholarship opportunities** allow coaching ministers to get the training they need without jeopardizing their financial stability, which is crucial given the often lower salaries in full-time ministry.

- **Chaplain (Career Track)**: Full-time chaplains serve in **military**, **healthcare**, **prisons**, and **corporate environments**. They often oversee entire **spiritual care programs**, engage in **crisis intervention**, and provide **emotional and spiritual support** to large groups. Full-time chaplains generally require extensive **chaplaincy education**, such as **Clinical Pastoral Education (CPE)**, along with certification. Since the cost of CPE programs and chaplain certification can be high, **donation-supported schools** offer chaplains the training they need without the financial strain of high tuition costs.

**Study Requirement for Career Ministers**: Full-time ministers often pursue **advanced theological degrees** and **professional certifications**. These require significant time and financial commitment, but **affordable programs** and **donation-supported institutions** help full-time ministers avoid accumulating debt. Given the lower salaries typically associated with ministry work, low-cost credentialing options are essential for those in full-time ministry to remain financially stable.

## The Importance of Donation-Supported Ministry Training

Across all tracks—**volunteer**, **part-time**, and **full-time**—**donation-supported ministry training schools** play a crucial role in ensuring that individuals can pursue their calling without taking on significant financial burdens. For **volunteers** and **part-time ministers**, the ability to receive **low-cost credentials** ensures that they can serve effectively while maintaining other jobs or responsibilities. For **full-time career ministers**, who often face **lower salaries** than those in other professions, **debt-free education** through scholarship-supported institutions is critical to their long-term sustainability in ministry.

By supporting these donation-based schools, the broader Christian community helps **mobilize more leaders**, making it possible for people of all economic backgrounds to serve in ministry. This approach reflects the **New Testament church**, where ministry roles were filled by individuals from diverse backgrounds, united in their calling to serve God and their communities

# Officiant Role

## The Role of the Officiant in Christianity

### Introduction

In Christianity, an officiant plays a special role in leading key life events like weddings, funerals, baptisms, and other celebrations. The officiant acts as a *diakonos*—a servant leader who helps connect people to God during these important moments. Ministry Sciences looks at how officiants serve their communities by overseeing ceremonies, teaching biblical truths, and giving blessings.

Officiants don't always have to be full-time ministers, but their work is essential to the Christian community. Whether they're helping couples exchange vows or offering comfort at a funeral, officiants bring a spiritual focus to these events, ensuring they honor God and the people involved.

**Biblical Roots of the Officiant Role**

The idea of the officiant goes all the way back to the Bible, where leaders often led ceremonies and gave blessings. One early example is Melchizedek, a priest who blessed Abram (later Abraham) and shared bread and wine with him. This story, found in **Genesis 14:18-20**, shows how officiants have always helped people connect with God's blessings.

"Melchizedek, king of Salem, brought out bread and wine. He was a priest of God Most High. He blessed him, and said, 'Blessed be Abram of God Most High, possessor of heaven and earth. Blessed be God Most High, who has delivered your enemies into your hand.' Abram gave him a tenth of all."

In the Old Testament, other leaders like Aaron and Samuel also acted as officiants, leading ceremonies and offering prayers on behalf of their communities. **Leviticus 10:11** shows how priests were tasked with teaching the people:

"You are to teach the children of Israel all the statutes which Yahweh has spoken to them by Moses" (WEB).

**Officiants in the New Testament**

The role of the officiant continues in the New Testament, where key figures like John the Baptist and the apostles led baptisms, performed ceremonies, and gave blessings.

- **John the Baptist** baptized many, including Jesus, showing how baptism is a key part of an officiant's duties.
  "Jesus came from Galilee to the Jordan to John, to be baptized by him" (**Matthew 3:13**).

- **The apostles** also acted as officiants when they led the early church. **Acts 2:42** describes their activities:
  "They continued steadfastly in the apostles' teaching and fellowship, in the breaking of bread, and prayer."

- **Philip the Evangelist** baptized the Ethiopian eunuch, showing another example of an officiant helping someone connect with God. (**Acts 8:35-38**).

These examples show that throughout history, officiants have played a critical role in connecting people to God through ceremonies and blessings.

**Early Christian Leadership and Modern Officiants**

When Christianity first began, leadership roles were often voluntary. Many early Christian leaders, like the Apostle Paul, had regular jobs. Paul, for example, was a tentmaker. This allowed him to support himself while spreading the Gospel. **Acts 18:3** says:

"Because he was of the same trade, he stayed with them and worked, for by trade they were tent makers."

Early Christian communities were supported by volunteers who opened their homes and helped traveling ministers. Over time, however, church leadership became more formal, and volunteer roles decreased. But today, programs like the **Officiant Ministry Program** at Christian Leaders Institute are bringing back the volunteer ministry model, allowing Christians to serve as officiants in their local communities.

**The Officiant Ministry Program**

This program helps train Christians who feel called to lead ceremonies like weddings, baptisms, and funerals. The program provides training and official recognition for these roles, allowing individuals to serve their communities with confidence. Some of the main duties of an officiant include:

- **Teaching the Word of God:** Officiants are responsible for teaching biblical principles and leading others in faith.
  "You are to teach the children of Israel all the statutes" (**Leviticus 10:11**).

- **Leading Worship and Prayer:** Officiants guide the congregation in worship, prayer, and Bible reading.
  "Oh come, let us sing to Yahweh. Let us make a joyful noise" (**Psalm 95:1**).

- **Performing Ceremonies:** Officiants conduct weddings, funerals, baptisms, and other key events.
  "For this cause a man will leave his father and his mother and will join with his wife, and they will be one flesh" (**Genesis 2:24**).

- **Providing Comfort and Pastoral Care:** Officiants offer support and guidance to people in times of joy or sorrow.
  "Is any among you sick? Let him call for the elders of the assembly, and let them pray over him" (**James 5:14**).

## Officiants in Today's World

Officiants today continue the tradition of service and leadership established in the Bible. Whether they are leading a wedding, baptizing a new believer, or comforting a grieving family, their work is essential to the Christian community.

Through programs like the Christian Leaders Institute, people can receive training to become officiants. The program offers specific tracks, such as **Wedding Officiant**, **Funeral Officiant**, and **Romance Officiant**, so individuals can serve in the areas where they feel called. Once trained, officiants receive certificates, letters of good standing, and other credentials to show they are prepared to serve their communities.

## Conclusion

The role of the officiant is important in Christianity because it helps people connect with God during key moments in life. From the early days of the Bible to today, officiants have served by leading ceremonies, offering prayers, and providing comfort. Programs like the Officiant Ministry Program allow Christians to continue this tradition of service, fulfilling their calling and making a difference in their communities.

## Further Reading:

1. **"Building a StoryBrand: Clarify Your Message So Customers Will Listen"** by Donald Miller
   This book explores how to communicate clearly, helping people connect with the deeper message of faith and service.

2. **"Jesus Our Priest: A Christian Approach to the Priesthood of Christ"** by Gerald O'Collins and Michael Keenan Jones
   A deep dive into the priestly role of Jesus and how it informs Christian leadership today.

# Minister Role

## Ministry Sciences Study of the Role of the Minister

### Introduction

In the last chapter, we looked at the ministry officiant, a person with specialized training to conduct ceremonies like weddings. But a minister's role goes beyond officiating; ministers are called to lead, preach, teach, and care for their congregations. In this chapter, we'll explore what it means to be a licensed or ordained minister and the different responsibilities they take on.

## The Story of Barnabas, Paul, and John Mark

The story of Barnabas, Paul, and John Mark in the Bible shows how ministers are raised up and trained. Paul, called by Jesus on the road to Damascus, became one of the most important ministers in early Christianity. He didn't start alone though. **Acts 9:26-27** shows that Barnabas mentored Paul, helping him grow as a minister.

Barnabas and Paul went on missionary trips together, and John Mark, a young minister, joined them. However, John Mark abandoned the mission partway through (Acts 13:13). Later, when Paul wanted to go on another journey, he didn't want to bring John Mark along, thinking he wasn't ready. Barnabas disagreed, and the two went separate ways, with Barnabas taking John Mark and Paul choosing Silas as his companion (Acts 15:36-40).

This story teaches us that ministers need time and guidance to grow. John Mark wasn't ready at first, but later Paul recognized him as a valuable helper in ministry (2 Timothy 4:11). Just like John Mark, many ministers need nurturing and experience before fully stepping into their roles.

## The Role of the Minister

Today, ministers take on a variety of roles. Some are volunteers, while others are part-time or full-time leaders in the church. Here are some key responsibilities of a minister, though not all ministers will do everything on this list. For example, a senior pastor will have a different role than a youth minister.

**1. Moral Integrity**

Ministers must live with honesty and integrity. The Bible tells us that leaders in the church should be "above reproach" (1 Timothy 3:2). This means they must show good character and make wise choices, setting an example for others.

**2. Sound Doctrine**

Ministers should be knowledgeable about the Bible and able to teach it correctly. They must explain biblical truths clearly and help people understand how to live out their faith (Titus 1:9).

**3. Teaching and Mentoring**

A big part of being a minister is teaching and mentoring others. Ministers help people grow in their understanding of Scripture and guide them in applying biblical principles in everyday life.

**4. Managing the Household**

The Bible says that ministers should manage their own households well (1 Timothy 3:4-5). This shows that a leader's personal life reflects their ability to lead the church effectively.

**5. Pastoral Care and Counseling**

Ministers offer support and care during difficult times. They might visit someone in the hospital, counsel those going through a tough time, or pray with families dealing with loss.

**6. Community Engagement**

Ministers often lead outreach efforts in the community, whether that's through food drives, working with the homeless, or starting after-school programs. They act as the hands and feet of Jesus, showing love to those in need.

**7. Preaching**

One of the most important roles of a minister is preaching. This is when ministers share the message of the Gospel, challenge the congregation to grow, and offer hope through God's Word.

**8. Evangelism**

Ministers are responsible for sharing the Gospel with others, both inside and outside the church. They lead efforts to bring more people to Christ and make sure the church stays focused on its mission of spreading the Good News.

**9. Leadership and Governance**

In many cases, ministers help run the church or ministry. This includes managing staff, leading the vision of the church, and overseeing financial decisions. Good leadership is essential to keeping the church healthy and effective.

## Qualifications from Titus 1 and 1 Timothy 3

The Bible gives clear guidelines for the qualities a minister should have. **Titus 1:5-9** and **1 Timothy 3:1-7** tell us that a minister should be:

- **Above reproach** – They live with integrity and set a good example.
- **Able to teach** – They know the Bible and can explain it well.
- **Self-controlled** – They show discipline in their actions and decisions.
- **Hospitable** – They are welcoming and care for others.
- **Not quick-tempered** – They are patient and calm under pressure.

These qualities are important because they show that a minister can be trusted to lead others in faith.

## Preaching and Teaching

Ministers are called to preach and teach God's Word. This includes delivering sermons, leading

Bible studies, and mentoring individuals. Teaching others about God is a key part of a minister's role because it helps people grow in their faith and understanding.

Preaching is more than just giving a speech. It's about communicating God's truth in a way that challenges, encourages, and inspires. Good preaching makes Scripture come alive and helps people see how it applies to their lives today.

**Evangelism and Multiplication**

Ministers are also called to share the Gospel with others. Evangelism is about spreading the message of Jesus and inviting people to follow Him. But beyond sharing the Gospel, ministers also help raise up other leaders. They mentor and train people to become future leaders in the church.

**Community Leadership and Engagement**

Ministers are often leaders in their communities, not just within the church. They work to make a positive impact by getting involved in local issues, helping those in need, and partnering with others to bring about positive change. Community engagement allows ministers to show God's love in practical ways.

**Governing and Movement Leadership**

Many ministers also help lead the organizational side of the church. This includes creating budgets, managing programs, and developing long-term strategies to help the church grow and thrive. These responsibilities help ensure that the church operates smoothly and stays focused on its mission.

**Conclusion**

The role of the minister is wide-ranging, covering everything from preaching and teaching to caring for people and managing church operations. Ministers are called to serve their congregations with integrity, love, and wisdom. Whether they are preaching a sermon or helping a family in need, ministers are vital to the life of the church and the spiritual growth of God's people.

**For Further Reading:**

1. **"The Minister as Shepherd"** by Charles Edward Jefferson – A classic look at what it means to lead and care for a congregation.
2. **"Pastoral Ministry: How to Shepherd Biblically"** by John MacArthur – A guide to understanding the biblical responsibilities of a pastor.
3. **"The Imperfect Pastor"** by Zack Eswine – A book about finding joy in serving as a pastor, even with all its challenges.

# Coaching Minister Role

**The Role of the Coaching Minister: A Ministry Sciences Response to the Life Coaching Field**

In a world filled with confusion, brokenness, and a constant search for meaning, many people are turning to **life coaching** for guidance, clarity, and direction. Life coaching, a rapidly growing field, emphasizes personal growth, goal-setting, and overcoming obstacles. But it often leaves something significant out: the spiritual dimension of life. In contrast, the **Coaching Minister** not only incorporates personal development but grounds it in biblical principles, spiritual wisdom, and the redemptive power of God.

**Ministry Sciences**, the study of integrating faith, ministry, and practical tools, offers a powerful framework for Coaching Ministers. It equips them with training similar to life coaching while rooting them in spiritual guidance. Unlike secular life coaching, Coaching Ministers are deeply connected to their ministry work and driven by a calling to help others grow in their relationship with God while addressing their life's challenges.

This article explores the contrast between life coaching and the Coaching Minister role and how **Ministry Science** sstudies show the importance of grounding coaching within a faith-based framework.

## The Rise of Life Coaching: Secular Guidance Without God

In recent years, life coaching has emerged as a popular alternative to therapy and counseling, focusing on helping individuals set and achieve personal and professional goals. Life coaches offer guidance in areas such as career development, relationships, health, and personal fulfillment. Their methods include goal-setting, accountability, motivation, and encouragement—an approach that many find valuable in a fast-paced, high-stress world.

However, the life coaching industry tends to operate from a secular standpoint, often excluding any reference to God, spiritual growth, or the deeper existential questions of life. It centers on individual autonomy and success, driven by the belief that people can solve their own problems through personal empowerment.

This secular approach, while helpful to some degree, can leave people feeling spiritually empty. It addresses surface-level goals but doesn't delve into the more profound aspects of meaning, purpose, and the role of faith in personal growth. People seeking life coaching may find practical solutions to their problems but often lack the spiritual nourishment they need to thrive holistically.

## The Coaching Minister: Rooted in Ministry, Empowered by Coaching Training

Enter the **Coaching Minister**—an alternative response that combines the best aspects of life coaching with the depth and richness of ministry. The Coaching Minister is not just focused on personal success but is grounded in helping people align their lives with God's will, grow in faith, and find joy and purpose through spiritual transformation. This role is both **pastoral** and **practical**, offering a holistic approach that incorporates faith into every aspect of personal growth.

Here's where **Ministry Sciences** comes in. Ministry Sciences recognizes that while secular approaches can provide valuable tools for personal development, they fall short when they leave out the spiritual dimension. Ministry Sciences studies how Coaching Ministers are empowered by ministry training **and** coaching methodologies, grounding their approach in biblical principles and the work of the Holy Spirit.

**How is this different from life coaching?**

1. **The Foundation in Faith:**
   Life coaching typically starts with the premise that individuals have the power to determine their destiny. Coaching Ministers, however, begin with the understanding that humans are created by God, redeemed through Christ, and guided by the Holy Spirit. They believe that true fulfillment comes not just from achieving personal goals but from aligning one's life with God's design and purpose.
   *Proverbs 3:5-6 (NIV): "Trust in the Lord with all your heart and lean not on your own understanding; in all your ways submit to him, and he will make your paths straight."*
   Coaching Ministers ground their practice in scripture, encouraging people to trust in God's plan rather than relying solely on their abilities.

2. **Spiritual Growth as a Core Objective:**
   Life coaching is centered around success, whether in business, relationships, or health. While these are important, Coaching Ministers are primarily concerned with **spiritual growth**. Their objective is to help individuals deepen their relationship with God, become more Christ-like, and live in alignment with biblical principles.
   **Ministry Sciences** studies show that people's well-being is not complete unless their spiritual life is thriving. This is where Coaching Ministers offer something life coaching does not—spiritual transformation alongside practical growth.

3. **Coaching Ministers Are Pastors First, Coaches Second:**
   Coaching Ministers are trained and credentialed in ministry, often having pastoral responsibilities such as preaching, teaching, and providing pastoral care. While life coaches typically have no formal spiritual role, Coaching Ministers approach every session with the heart of a pastor. Their guidance is not just about achieving a specific goal but about fostering spiritual wholeness in every area of life.
   *Proverbs 20:5 (NIV): "The purposes of a person's heart are deep waters, but one who has insight draws them out."*
   A Coaching Minister helps individuals discover their purpose not merely for personal success but for fulfilling God's plan for their life.

4. **Biblical Wisdom Over Secular Theories:**
   Life coaches draw from psychology, motivational techniques, and personal development

theories. Coaching Ministers, on the other hand, turn to the Bible as their primary source of wisdom. The Book of Proverbs, for example, is rich with guidance on navigating life's challenges and making wise decisions.
**Proverbs 4:7 (NIV): "The beginning of wisdom is this: Get wisdom. Though it cost all you have, get understanding."**
The Coaching Minister helps individuals grow in **wisdom**, which includes not just knowing what to do but how to live a life that honors God.

5   **Coaching Ministers Address the Soul's Needs:**
    Secular life coaching focuses on achieving external goals, but Coaching Ministers recognize that people are more than their ambitions. They are **souls**, created in the image of God, who need spiritual guidance, healing, and encouragement. Coaching Ministers integrate prayer, scriptural reflection, and spiritual direction into their sessions, addressing the whole person—body, mind, and spirit.
    **Ministry Sciences** emphasizes this holistic approach, studying how spiritual practices, grounded in faith, contribute to long-lasting personal and spiritual development.

## Ministry Sciences and Coaching Training: The Best of Both Worlds

**Ministry Sciences** offers a framework for understanding how the Coaching Minister role is both grounded in ministry and empowered with coaching training. Coaching Ministers undergo rigorous training in both theology and ministry practice while also learning coaching techniques that focus on active listening, goal setting, and motivation. This integration allows them to serve in a way that is **spiritually deep** and **practically effective**.

**Ministry Sciences** recognizes that Coaching Ministers can draw from life coaching methods—such as setting goals, creating action plans, and tracking progress—but they do so with a spiritual foundation that life coaches often lack. This makes Coaching Ministers unique in their ability to offer both **spiritual wisdom** and **practical guidance**, creating lasting transformation in the lives of those they serve.

**The Core Components of Ministry Sciences for Coaching Ministers:**

1   **Biblical Foundations:** Coaching Ministers are rooted in scripture, using the Bible as the ultimate guide for wisdom and decision-making.

2   **Coaching Techniques:** Ministry Sciences incorporates the best practices from the coaching field, such as goal-setting, accountability, and motivational strategies. Coaching Ministers use these tools, but always within a context of faith and spiritual growth.

3   **Spiritual Empowerment:** Coaching Ministers are equipped by the Holy Spirit. They pray with and for their disciples/clients, seeking God's guidance at every step.

4   **Holistic Focus:** Ministry Sciences ensures that Coaching Ministers address not just the goals of their clients but their overall well-being, including emotional, relational, and spiritual health.

5   **Credentialing:** Coaching Ministers are not just trained in coaching techniques but also **credentialed as ministers**, often through programs like the Christian Leaders Alliance. This allows them to serve as both spiritual leaders and life coaches, offering a deeper level of service.

## Ministry Sciences: A Study of Spiritual and Practical Integration

Ministry Sciences studies the role of Coaching Ministers and explores how spiritual coaching differs from secular life coaching. One of its core tenets is that **spirituality cannot be separated from personal development**. Individuals are not merely biological or psychological beings — they are spiritual beings created in God's image. Therefore, coaching that excludes this reality is incomplete.

Coaching Ministers are equipped to help people grow spiritually while addressing their personal goals. Whether guiding someone through a career change, helping with relational struggles, or working on personal development, they ensure that spiritual alignment with God's will is the foundation for every decision.

**Non-Directive, Directive, and Semi-Directive Coaching**: Ministry Sciences emphasizes that Coaching Ministers, much like life coaches, use different techniques depending on the individual's needs. However, they always bring a ministry perspective into the coaching:

- **Non-Directive Coaching** encourages clients to draw out their own insights, grounded in the belief that the Holy Spirit is at work within them (Proverbs 20:5).
- **Directive Coaching** provides clear, biblically based instructions when needed, ensuring that individuals receive practical and spiritual guidance (Proverbs 6:6-8).
- **Semi-Directive Coaching** offers a balance, allowing for both personal discovery and spiritual direction, trusting in God's guidance for every step (Proverbs 3:5-6).

## Empowering Ministers Through Coaching Training

The role of the Coaching Minister is unique because it blends **ministerial authority** with modern coaching methods. At **Christian Leaders Institute**, Coaching Ministers receive both theological and coaching training, preparing them to offer more than just practical advice — they offer spiritual transformation.

- **Coaching Ministers** are trained to help individuals **align their goals with God's will**, to **discern spiritual challenges**, and to use **coaching tools** to help clients make meaningful, lasting changes.
- This training equips them to serve in a variety of settings — whether in churches, nonprofits, or community organizations — where the need for both spiritual and personal guidance is great.

## Conclusion: A Call to Consider Ministry Sciences and Coaching Ministry

In a world where secular life coaching may offer guidance but lacks depth, the **Coaching**

**Minister** provides a meaningful alternative. Rooted in ministry, empowered by coaching training, and grounded in **Ministry Sciences**, Coaching Ministers bring a holistic approach that addresses the mind, body, and soul.

For those seeking a career or calling in helping others, **Ministry Sciences** offers an exciting and fulfilling path—one that combines the best of coaching with the transformative power of ministry. Coaching Ministers are not just goal-setters but soul-carers, leading people toward lives of joy, purpose, and deep connection with God.

**Further Reading:**

- "Coaching for Christian Leaders" by Chad Hall
- "Proverbs: Wisdom That Works" by Raymond C. Ortlund Jr.
- "Faith-Based Coaching: The Ministry of the Christian Coach" by Sam McFadden

This is not just about offering advice; it's about **life transformation**—grounded in God's Word and empowered by the Holy Spirit.

# Chaplain Role

## The Role of the Chaplain Minister in Ministry Sciences: A Study of Spiritual Care and Support

### Introduction to the Chaplain Minister Role

The **Chaplain Minister** serves as a vital bridge between spiritual care and real-world support, bringing the presence of God into diverse environments. From workplaces to public service settings, hospitals to virtual spaces, Chaplain Ministers play a pivotal role in providing spiritual guidance, comfort, and counseling to those in need. Unlike traditional pastoral roles confined to church settings, Chaplain Ministers expand their reach by integrating principles of **Ministry Sciences** to offer both **in-person and online** chaplaincy services. They are trained not only in foundational pastoral care but also in the specific needs of various communities, combining **ministry and science** to effectively minister in a wide range of settings.

This article contrasts the role of the Chaplain Minister with traditional chaplaincy and explores how the Chaplain Minister integrates **Ministry Sciences**—a field that studies how spiritual care, evidence-based practices, and interdisciplinary approaches can be combined for holistic ministry.

### Core Responsibilities of the Chaplain Minister

#### 1. Presence and Support

A key aspect of the Chaplain Minister's role is providing **presence and spiritual support** in diverse environments. Whether in a corporate office, a hospital, a police department, or an online chat-based ministry, the Chaplain Minister offers a **calming and spiritual presence**, helping people navigate personal challenges with God's guidance.

- **Workplace Chaplaincy**: In corporate or industrial settings, Chaplain Ministers help employees handle stress, conflict, or personal crises by being a nonjudgmental and approachable source of spiritual care. They listen to concerns, provide prayer, and offer spiritual counsel that helps foster a healthier, more compassionate work environment.

- **Public Service Chaplaincy**: Chaplain Ministers who serve police officers, firefighters, and other public service workers provide emotional and spiritual support to those who encounter high-stress situations. They help these first responders process trauma, build emotional resilience, and offer support during crises.

- **Online Chaplaincy**: The rise of digital ministry has allowed Chaplain Ministers to extend their reach globally. They offer real-time spiritual support through chat-based ministries, emails, or social media engagement, creating safe virtual spaces for individuals to seek spiritual guidance, prayer, and comfort.

## 2. Spiritual Guidance and Counseling

Chaplain Ministers offer **spiritual guidance and counseling**, providing care to individuals dealing with illness, grief, and personal crises. Their training enables them to provide biblically grounded counsel and emotional support, addressing both the spiritual and psychological needs of individuals.

- **Illness and Grief**: In hospitals and hospice care, Chaplain Ministers pray with the sick, offering comfort and hope grounded in scripture. For those grieving, they provide compassionate counsel, helping families process loss through biblically based hope and memorial services that honor the life of the deceased.

- **Crisis Intervention**: In times of unexpected tragedy, such as natural disasters or accidents, Chaplain Ministers are on the front lines, offering immediate spiritual and emotional support to individuals and communities. Their long-term support through follow-up care helps individuals and communities recover emotionally and spiritually from the trauma.

## 3. Conducting Religious Services

Chaplain Ministers are also responsible for conducting **religious ceremonies** such as weddings, funerals, and invocations at public events. Their ability to blend traditional religious services with the specific needs of those they serve allows for customized and meaningful ceremonies.

- **Weddings**: Chaplain Ministers work closely with couples to officiate personalized wedding ceremonies grounded in Christian values. They also offer pre-marital counseling to help couples build a strong, faith-centered marriage.

- **Funerals**: In funeral and memorial services, Chaplain Ministers offer spiritual comfort to grieving families and friends. They provide personalized services that honor the deceased's faith and life, while also offering words of hope based on biblical teachings about eternal life.

- **Public Ceremonies**: Chaplain Ministers are often invited to lead invocations, prayers, and religious observances at public events, fostering spiritual unity and community engagement.

## 4. Building and Maintaining Relationships

Building **trust and rapport** with those they serve is essential for Chaplain Ministers. By establishing strong relationships in their communities—whether in fire departments, hospitals, or online—they become a trusted source of spiritual support.

- **Fire and Police Departments**: Through regular visits to fire stations or police departments, Chaplain Ministers build relationships with first responders, offering them a safe space to express their struggles and seek spiritual counsel.

- **Community Engagement**: By actively participating in community events and volunteer programs, Chaplain Ministers create a visible presence that promotes a culture of care, unity, and spiritual growth.

## 5. Training and Education

Continuous learning is a key part of the Chaplain Minister's role. By engaging in ongoing education in **chaplaincy, counseling, theology, and Ministry Sciences**, Chaplain Ministers ensure that their care remains relevant and effective.

- **Chaplaincy Programs**: Chaplain Ministers are encouraged to take advanced courses in specific areas like healthcare or military chaplaincy, allowing them to address the unique spiritual needs of those in specialized environments.

- **Ministry Sciences Workshops**: Participating in **Ministry Sciences** workshops equips Chaplain Ministers with interdisciplinary tools and evidence-based practices, helping them offer holistic care that integrates theology, psychology, and leadership development.

## 6. Adaptability and Innovation

In an ever-changing world, Chaplain Ministers must be adaptable and innovative, integrating new technologies and creative approaches to ministry. The rise of **digital chaplaincy** has opened new avenues for ministry that extend beyond traditional in-person settings.

- **Virtual Chaplaincy**: Chaplain Ministers offer virtual spiritual support through social media, video conferencing, and digital platforms. Whether through online worship services or support groups, they meet people where they are—physically or digitally.

- **Hybrid Ministry Models**: Combining in-person and online chaplaincy models allows

Chaplain Ministers to offer flexible, accessible care that reaches a broader audience.

## 7. Ethical and Confidential Practice

Chaplain Ministers must adhere to the highest ethical standards, ensuring confidentiality and maintaining trust with those they serve. Whether counseling individuals or conducting public services, ethical practice is paramount to their role.

- **Confidentiality**: Chaplain Ministers create a safe environment where individuals can share personal concerns without fear of judgment or breach of privacy. They are trained to handle sensitive information with care, especially when working with first responders, patients, or online clients.

- **Ethical Decision-Making**: In situations where ethical dilemmas arise, Chaplain Ministers rely on biblical principles and ethical frameworks to navigate these complexities, ensuring that their decisions reflect integrity and Christian values.

## 8. Coordination with Other Service Providers

Chaplain Ministers often work in collaboration with **medical staff, social workers, and emergency personnel**, providing holistic care that addresses spiritual, emotional, and practical needs. By coordinating with these service providers, Chaplain Ministers ensure that the people they serve receive comprehensive support.

- **Interdisciplinary Collaboration**: Whether in a hospital or fire department, Chaplain Ministers join interdisciplinary teams to offer spiritual care as part of a larger support system that includes medical and psychological services.

- **Resource Referrals**: Chaplain Ministers help connect individuals with additional resources, such as mental health services or social support networks, offering a holistic approach to care.

# Ministry Sciences: A Study of Chaplaincy's Integration with Evidence-Based Practices

In **Ministry Sciences**, the role of the Chaplain Minister is studied as a dynamic and evolving form of ministry that blends spiritual care with practical, evidence-based approaches. Ministry Sciences affirms that while spiritual care is deeply rooted in theology and biblical principles, it can also benefit from the tools and insights of other disciplines, such as **psychology, sociology, and leadership development**.

- **Holistic Ministry**: Ministry Sciences encourages Chaplain Ministers to approach their ministry holistically, addressing the spiritual, emotional, and physical needs of those they serve. This interdisciplinary perspective enriches their capacity to minister effectively in diverse settings.

- **Continuous Improvement**: A key tenet of Ministry Sciences is the commitment to continuous improvement. Chaplain Ministers are encouraged to evaluate their practices regularly, seeking feedback and applying the latest research to their ministry efforts.

## Conclusion: The Unique Role of the Chaplain Minister

The **Chaplain Minister** stands apart from traditional chaplaincy roles through their integration of **Ministry Sciences**, which equips them with a unique blend of spiritual authority and evidence-based practices. Their ability to minister in both **in-person and online settings** allows them to reach people where they are, offering comfort, guidance, and hope in times of need. By incorporating continuous learning, ethical practice, and interdisciplinary collaboration, Chaplain Ministers fulfill a vital role in today's world, ensuring that those they serve receive holistic, faith-based care that addresses the challenges of modern life.

**For Further Reading**:

- "**Chaplaincy: A Ministry of Presence**" by Winnifred Fallers Sullivan
- "**The Work of the Chaplain**" by Naomi K. Paget and Janet R. McCormack
- "**Hospital Chaplaincy in the Twenty-first Century: The Crisis of Spiritual Care**" by Christopher Swift
- "**Spiritual Care in Practice: Case Studies in Healthcare Chaplaincy**" by George Fitchett and Steve Nolan

# Credentialing Credibility

## The Marks of Minister Credentialing: A Historical Survey

## Introduction

For over two thousand years, minister credentialing has evolved in various forms across different Christian traditions, yet the foundational principles remain consistent. These principles aim to ensure that **officiants**, **ministers**, **coaching ministers**, and **chaplains** are **confident**, **competent**, and **credible** in their service. Ministry Sciences, in studying these processes, identifies essential elements of credentialing that provide a biblical, historical, and practical framework for evaluating, training, and endorsing ministry leaders.

## Essential Components of Minister Credentialing

Credentialing follows a structured path rooted in biblical principles, ensuring that ministers are well-prepared for their roles. These key components include:

1. **Victorious Walk with God**:
   Minister candidates must demonstrate a **victorious walk with God**, living a life transformed by the Holy Spirit and consistently aligned with biblical teachings. This

includes embodying the **fruits of the Spirit**, as outlined in Galatians 5:22-23:
*"But the fruit of the Spirit is love, joy, peace, patience, kindness, goodness, faith, gentleness, and self-control. Against such things there is no law."* (Galatians 5:22-23 WEB)
Ministers are called to live out these virtues daily, overcoming challenges through faith in Christ, as stated in 1 John 5:4-5:
*"For whatever is born of God overcomes the world. This is the victory that has overcome the world: your faith."*
This victorious walk reflects spiritual maturity and leadership integrity, foundational for those called to serve others.

2. **Internal Call from God**:
An internal call is a deeply personal conviction that God has chosen an individual for ministry. This sense of purpose, often felt as a **divine calling**, aligns with the Apostle Paul's experience in Galatians 1:15-16:
*"But when it was the good pleasure of God, who separated me from my mother's womb and called me through his grace, to reveal his Son in me, that I might preach him among the Gentiles, I didn't immediately confer with flesh and blood."* (Galatians 1:15-16 WEB)
Ministry candidates must discern this internal calling through prayer and reflection, affirming their commitment to God's mission.

3. **External Call Recognized by Others**:
An **external call** occurs when the church or community acknowledges the candidate's calling, confirming their readiness for ministry. This affirmation is often formalized through the laying on of hands, as seen in Acts 13:2-3:
*"As they served the Lord and fasted, the Holy Spirit said, 'Separate Barnabas and Saul for me, for the work to which I have called them.' Then, when they had fasted and prayed and laid their hands on them, they sent them away."*
This recognition provides accountability and support, ensuring the candidate's gifts and calling are validated by trusted leaders.

4. **Credentialing by Churches or Christian Religious Societies**:
Ministerial credentialing has been a long-standing tradition, passed down from the **early church** through Catholic and Protestant denominations. Although the methods may vary, the essential elements—**divine calling**, **training**, and **endorsement**—remain consistent. Paul's instruction in 1 Timothy 4:14 highlights the importance of ordination:
*"Don't neglect the gift that is in you, which was given to you by prophecy, with the laying on of the hands of the elders."* (1 Timothy 4:14 WEB)
Churches and religious societies play a vital role in overseeing the credentialing process, ensuring that ministers are trained and spiritually prepared to lead.

# Marks of a Religious Society Credible to Credential Ministers

For a religious society to credential ministers effectively, it must uphold the following marks of credibility:

1. **Biblical Statement of Faith (Confessional Succession)**:
   The society must hold to a **biblical statement of faith**, ensuring doctrinal purity and alignment with historic Christian teachings. Paul instructed Timothy to adhere to sound doctrine:
   *"Hold the pattern of sound words which you have heard from me, in faith and love which is in Christ Jesus."* (2 Timothy 1:13-14 WEB)
   A firm confessional foundation guarantees that ministers are trained within a framework of sound theology.

2. **Appropriate Ministry Training Program (Competency Succession)**:
   Ministerial training must be appropriate for the specific role, whether for a **wedding officiant** or an ordained pastor. Ephesians 4:11-12 emphasizes the importance of equipping leaders:
   *"He gave some to be apostles; and some, prophets; and some, evangelists; and some, shepherds and teachers; for the perfecting of the saints, to the work of serving, to the building up of the body of Christ."*
   A robust training program provides candidates with both **theological knowledge** and **practical ministry skills**.

3. **Local Endorsement (Community Succession)**:
   Candidates must receive endorsements from their community, affirming their Christian walk and character. In Acts 6:3, the early church sought leaders of good reputation:
   *"Therefore select from among you, brothers, seven men of good report, full of the Holy Spirit and of wisdom, whom we may appoint over this business."*
   Endorsements reflect the candidate's credibility and trustworthiness, confirming their readiness for ministry.

4. **Public Credentials (Recognition Succession)**:
   Religious societies must provide **public credentials**, such as certificates or ordination documents, recognizing the candidate's role. In Acts 13:2-3, Paul and Barnabas were publicly commissioned:
   *"Separate Barnabas and Saul for me, for the work to which I have called them."*
   Public credentials affirm the minister's standing, giving them authority and recognition in the Christian community.

## Volunteer, Part-Time, and Career Track Ministry Roles

In Ministry Sciences, individuals can serve as **volunteers**, **part-time**, or **full-time ministers**, providing flexibility for people with diverse life circumstances. The level of commitment and training required varies based on the chosen track.

1. **Volunteer Roles**:
   Volunteer ministers often serve in smaller churches or specialized ministries without

compensation. Training is typically **short-term** and focused on practical skills, and donation-supported training schools ensure that volunteers can access education **debt-free**. This helps volunteers focus on their calling without financial strain.

**Example**: A volunteer **officiant** may need minimal training to perform weddings or baptisms, but donation-supported programs make this training accessible without placing a financial burden on the candidate.

2. **Part-Time Roles**:
Part-time ministers may serve in bi-vocational settings, balancing ministry with other employment. **Moderate training** is required, often involving **certifications** or **seminary courses**. Affordable education options are essential for part-time ministers, as many work without full salaries from their ministry roles.

**Example**: A part-time **chaplain** may require certification in pastoral care but can access this training through **donation-supported schools**, allowing them to serve while maintaining other employment.

3. **Career Track**:
Full-time ministers dedicate their entire professional lives to ministry and require **extensive training**, often through **theological degrees** or **professional development programs**. However, full-time ministers typically earn lower salaries, making affordable training essential to avoid debt. Donation-supported ministry schools enable full-time ministers to receive the necessary education without financial hardship.

**Example**: A **minister of the word** may pursue an **MDiv** or similar degree but rely on **low-cost credentialing** programs to remain financially stable, especially when entering a field with modest salaries.

## The Role of Donation-Supported Ministry Schools

**Donation-supported ministry training schools** are vital to ensuring that individuals can pursue their calling without accumulating debt, especially in **volunteer** and **part-time roles**. These schools make **low-cost credentials** accessible to those with a heart for ministry but limited financial resources. This approach allows ministers to focus on their service, whether in a **volunteer** capacity or in **full-time ministry**, where salaries may be lower.

- **For volunteers**, donation-supported schools ensure that they can receive the training needed to serve their communities effectively without worrying about financial burdens.
- **For full-time ministers**, **debt-free education** is crucial, given that many ministry roles offer lower compensation compared to secular careers. Low-cost credentialing allows these ministers to focus on their work without being weighed down by student loan payments.

By providing affordable education, **donation-supported institutions** play a key role in **mobilizing more leaders** for the Kingdom, ensuring that financial constraints do not hinder those called to serve.

# Conclusion: The Importance of Minister Credentialing

Credentialing processes across different Christian traditions ensure that ministers are equipped and affirmed in their calling. Through **internal and external calls**, rigorous **training**, and **community endorsement**, minister candidates are prepared to serve with confidence and credibility. Whether they are volunteers or full-time leaders, ministers are shaped by these processes, reflecting the biblical model of leadership development. **Donation-supported training schools** play a crucial role in making this journey accessible to all, ensuring that financial barriers do not prevent individuals from answering their call to ministry.

# Suggested Readings

To gain a deeper understanding of minister credentialing, its historical context, and practical applications, the following books and resources provide a well-rounded exploration of ministry leadership and credentialing processes:

**General Ministry and Leadership**

1. "The Complete Guide to Christian Denominations" by Ron Rhodes
   This book offers a broad overview of various Christian denominations, explaining their beliefs, history, and approaches to ministerial leadership.

2. "Pastoral Ministry: How to Shepherd Biblically" by John MacArthur
   An excellent guide for those entering pastoral ministry, offering biblical insights and practical advice on how to shepherd a congregation effectively.

3. "The Mentor Leader: Secrets to Building People and Teams that Win Consistently" by Tony Dungy
   While not directly about credentialing, this book provides valuable lessons on leadership and mentorship, which are critical elements of effective ministry.

**Historical and Theological Perspectives**

1. "The Story of Christian Theology: Twenty Centuries of Tradition and Reform" by Roger E. Olson
   A comprehensive history of Christian theology, offering insights into how ministerial roles and credentialing have evolved over time.

2. "Ordained Women in the Early Church: A Documentary History" by Kevin Madigan and Carolyn Osiek
   This resource explores the historical role of women in ministry and provides valuable primary source material on early Christian credentialing practices for women.

3. "The Apostolic Fathers: Greek Texts and English Translations" by Michael W. Holmes
   An essential collection of early Christian writings that offer insight into how leadership

and ministry were organized in the early church.

## Credentialing and Church Governance

1. **"The Ministry of Helps: Finding Your Place in the Body of Christ"** by Buddy Bell
   This book provides a practical guide for those exploring various roles within church ministry, focusing on the importance of service and leadership within the local church.

2. **"The Complete Handbook of Christian Chaplain Ministry: A Faith-Based Approach to Caring in Institutions"** by John V. Purcell
   This book focuses on chaplaincy, covering the specific credentialing and training required for those in chaplain roles within hospitals, prisons, and the military.

3. **"Independent Catholicism: A Study of Independent Catholic Movements"** by Richard J. Mammana Jr.
   A study of how independent churches approach minister credentialing outside of traditional denominational structures, offering perspectives on non-denominational and ecumenical credentialing processes.

## Volunteer and Part-Time Ministry

1. **"Tentmaking: The Life and Work of Business as Missions"** by Patrick Lai
   This book explores how individuals can balance business or secular careers with ministry, an important topic for those in volunteer or part-time ministry roles.

2. **"Called to Serve: Essays for Elders and Deacons"** by Michael Jinkins
   A resource that focuses on the roles of elders and deacons, providing theological and practical advice for those serving in volunteer or part-time ministry positions.

## Ministry Training and Credentialing Resources

1. **"Church Administration: Creating Efficiency for Effective Ministry"** by Robert H. Welch
   Provides insights into the organizational aspects of ministry, emphasizing the importance of administration and structure in maintaining effective leadership.

2. **"Spiritual Leadership: Moving People on to God's Agenda"** by Henry Blackaby and Richard Blackaby
   Outlines the principles of spiritual leadership, focusing on how leaders can align themselves with God's will and help others grow spiritually.

3. **"Volunteer Church: Mobilizing Your Congregation for Growth and Effectiveness"** by Leith Anderson and Jill Fox
   A valuable resource for pastors and leaders who rely on volunteer ministries, offering strategies for training, mobilizing, and leading volunteer teams in the church.

# More Volunteer Minister Roles

## Volunteer Ministers in Specialized Topics: A Ministry Sciences Exploration

In the landscape of Christian ministry, volunteer and part-time ministers have historically played a critical role in building the Church and spreading the Gospel. These individuals, driven by a sense of calling, equipped with spiritual gifts, and trained in specialized ministry areas, have formed an army of ministers who thrive in their personal lives, marriages, and in serving their families, friends, churches, and communities. *Ministry Sciences*, as a discipline, seeks to study and understand this phenomenon, focusing particularly on the role and impact of volunteer and part-time ministers within the Christian tradition.

## The History of Volunteer Ministers in the Early Church

Before Christianity became the state religion under Emperor Constantine in 313 AD, the early Church was sustained by a vibrant community of volunteer ministers. These men and women were crucial in forming early Christian culture and contributed significantly to the Church's rapid expansion. One of the most important historical insights in *Ministry Sciences* is the role of non-paid, volunteer ministers in this era. Their sacrifice and commitment provided a strong foundation for the Church's growth and sustainability, long before professional clergy emerged.

## Biblical Examples of Volunteer Ministers

The New Testament provides several key examples of volunteer ministers who played foundational roles in the early Church:

- **Mission Ministers**: Paul, along with Priscilla and Aquila, serve as prime examples of volunteers who spread the Gospel and planted churches. These individuals dedicated their lives to advancing Christ's message without any expectation of financial compensation. Paul, in particular, supported his ministry through his work as a tentmaker.
  *"Greet Priscilla and Aquila, my fellow workers in Christ Jesus, who risked their necks for my life, to whom not only I give thanks, but also all the churches of the Gentiles."* (Romans 16:3-4, WEB)

- **Benefactor Minister Volunteers**: Philemon and Apphia were wealthy Christians who hosted a church in their home. Paul's letter to Philemon reveals how benefactor ministers provided essential resources for the Church's mission.
  *"And to our beloved Apphia, and Archippus our fellow soldier, and to the assembly in your house."* (Philemon 1:2, WEB)

- **Phoebe**: A prominent volunteer minister in the early Church, Phoebe was a "diakonos" (servant or minister) entrusted by Paul to deliver his letter to the Romans, and likely played a vital role in addressing the Church's questions.
  *"I commend to you Phoebe, our sister, who is a servant of the assembly that is at Cenchreae, that you receive her in the Lord in a way worthy of the saints, and that you*

*assist her in whatever matter she may need from you, for she herself also has been a helper of many, and of my own self."* (Romans 16:1-2, WEB)

## Early Church Examples of Volunteer Ministers

The early Church was sustained by volunteer ministers from all walks of life. Linus, for example, is mentioned as the first bishop of Rome after Peter, highlighting how many early Church leaders were unpaid and driven by a sense of calling.

- **Slaves as Ministers**: Pliny the Younger, a Roman governor, famously mentioned the torture of two female slaves referred to as "ministers" in his letters to Emperor Trajan. This example showcases the broad inclusivity of early Christian ministry, where even those in marginalized positions could serve in significant roles.

## The Philosophy of Volunteer Ministry

Volunteer ministry is deeply rooted in the organic and spiritual order established by God. The Apostle Paul highlighted the importance of voluntary leadership, starting within the family, as an essential qualification for Church leadership:

*"One who rules his own house well, having children in subjection with all reverence; (but if a man doesn't know how to rule his own house, how will he take care of the assembly of God?)"* (1 Timothy 3:4-5, WEB)

At a deeper level, volunteer ministry mirrors the natural rhythms of family life, where love and care are given freely. Just as family relationships are entered into and nurtured voluntarily, so too is ministry in the Church an outpouring of voluntary, sacrificial love.

## Specialized Roles of Early Volunteer Ministers

Volunteer ministers in the early Church took on a variety of specialized roles. One significant example was the rescue of abandoned female infants, who were often left to die in Roman society. Christian ministers not only saved these infants but raised them as Christians, many of whom later married pagans and converted them to the faith.

During times of plague, Christians cared for the sick, often risking their own lives. This ministry of care led to the development of hospitals and served as a powerful testimony to the compassion and commitment of early Christians.

## Historical References for Early Volunteer Minister Roles

1. **Gospel Spreaders** (like Paul and Barnabas): Paul and Barnabas are key figures in Acts 13, where they are sent out by the Holy Spirit from Antioch to spread the Gospel.
2. **Church Planters** (like Priscilla and Aquila): These leaders planted and supported churches, especially in Ephesus and Rome.
3. **Hosts of House Churches** (like Philemon and Apphia): Philemon and Apphia hosted early Christian gatherings in their home.

4 **Deacons** (like Phoebe): Phoebe was a deacon of the church at Cenchreae, assisting with various ministries.
5 **Bishops** (like Linus): Linus, the first bishop of Rome after Peter, played a role in overseeing the spread of Christianity.
6 **Catechists** (teachers of new converts): Clement of Alexandria led the Catechetical School of Alexandria.
7 **Exorcists** (those who cast out demons): Origen wrote about exorcists, defending their ministry as essential in the Church.
8 **Healers** (those who prayed for the sick): Early Christians were expected to pray for healing, as mentioned in *The Didache*.
9 **Intercessors** (those devoted to prayer): Tertullian emphasized the importance of intercessory prayer.
10 **Prophets** (those who spoke God's word to the community): Montanus, an early prophet, led a movement that emphasized prophecy in the Church.
11 **Scribes** (those who copied and distributed Scriptures): Tertius, mentioned in Romans 16:22, acted as Paul's scribe.
12 **Evangelists** (those who proclaimed the Gospel in new areas): Philip the Evangelist spread the Gospel to Samaria and the Ethiopian eunuch.
13 **Apologists** (defenders of the faith): Justin Martyr was an early Christian apologist.
14 **Charity Workers** (those who cared for the poor): Basil the Great founded hospitals and cared for the needy.
15 **Missionaries** (those who traveled to spread the Gospel): Patrick of Ireland is a well-known missionary example, although his story comes later in Church history.
16 **Lectors Officiants** (those who read Scripture in worship services): Cyprian of Carthage mentioned lectors in his letters.
17 **Psaltists Officiants** (those who led singing in worship): Ignatius of Antioch highlighted the role of singing in worship.
18 **Gravedigger Ministry** (those who buried the dead): The *Didascalia Apostolorum* detailed roles for caring for the dead.
19 **Chaplains** (those who ministered to prisoners): Peter's interactions with imprisoned Christians in Acts 12 shows the beginnings of prison ministry.
20 **Armorers** (those who provided for missionaries): Luke, as Paul's physician and companion, is an early example.
21 **Widows** (those who dedicated themselves to prayer): The *Apostolic Constitutions* described the role of widows in the Church.
22 **Deaconesses ministers**: Women like Theodora of Alexandria served in key roles.
23 **Almoners** (those who distributed alms): Laurence of Rome was known for his distribution of alms.
24 **Baptism Officiants**: Deaconesses were entrusted with baptizing women.
25 **Marriage Officiants**: Church leaders, such as Ignatius of Antioch, emphasized officiating marriages.
26 **Romance Pastoral Counseling**: Early leaders, including Clement of Alexandria, offered guidance on relationships and marriage

# Modern Equivalents of Early Christian Minister Roles

1. **Gospel Spreaders (like Paul and Barnabas):**
   **Today's Evangelists** – These individuals share the message of Jesus through preaching, online platforms, podcasts, and mission trips. They reach people outside the traditional church setting, often speaking to large crowds or creating digital content to spread the Gospel.

2. **Church Planters (like Priscilla and Aquila):**
   **Church Starters** – These leaders establish new congregations, especially in urban areas or regions where churches are less common. They focus on building faith communities from the ground up and meeting the unique needs of their neighborhoods.

3. **Hosts of House Churches (like Philemon and Apphia):**
   **Small Group Leaders** – These individuals open their homes or facilitate groups within churches for Bible studies, prayer meetings, and fellowship. They help foster personal growth and close-knit Christian communities.

4. **Deacons (like Phoebe):**
   **Ministry Coordinators** – They manage church operations and outreach efforts, organizing service projects, volunteer efforts, and programs that support the congregation and community, such as food pantries or charity events.

5. **Bishops (like Linus):**
   **Regional Church Leaders** – Today's equivalents might be denominational overseers, pastors of multi-site churches, or leaders in large organizations responsible for multiple congregations, ensuring that churches remain spiritually healthy and aligned with their mission.

6. **Catechists (teachers of new converts):**
   **Discipleship Trainers** – They teach new believers the basics of the Christian faith through classes, mentorship, or online courses, helping people grow in their knowledge of Christianity and how to live it out.

7. **Exorcists (those who cast out demons):**
   **Deliverance Ministers** – These ministers specialize in prayer and spiritual guidance for individuals experiencing spiritual oppression or distress, helping them find freedom through faith.

8. **Healers (those who prayed for the sick):**
   **Prayer and Healing Ministries** – These are groups or individuals who pray for physical, emotional, and spiritual healing, often working alongside medical professionals or in church healing services.

9. **Intercessors (those devoted to prayer):**
   **Prayer Warriors/Prayer Teams** – Dedicated prayer groups who meet regularly to pray for the needs of others, the church, and global concerns. They often organize prayer

chains or prayer vigils to cover specific events or crises.

10  **Prophets (those who spoke God's word to the community):**
Spiritual Advisors/Prophetic Leaders – These leaders provide guidance and insight based on a strong sense of hearing from God, often offering spiritual direction to individuals or congregations.

11  **Scribes (those who copied and distributed Scriptures):**
Content Creators/Church Media Teams – These people manage church communications, create digital resources like sermon notes, blogs, or social media posts, and help distribute important messages and teachings.

12  **Evangelists (those who proclaimed the Gospel in new areas):**
Missions Directors/Outreach Coordinators – They organize and lead efforts to spread the Christian message in their local communities or internationally, coordinating mission trips, community events, and outreach programs.

13  **Apologists (defenders of the faith):**
Christian Writers and Speakers – They engage in defending and explaining the Christian faith to the public, writing books, blogs, or participating in debates and discussions, addressing questions and challenges to Christianity.

14  **Charity Workers (those who cared for the poor and needy):**
Non-Profit Ministry Leaders – These leaders run organizations or church programs that provide for the needs of the underprivileged, such as food banks, shelters, and crisis response initiatives.

15  **Missionaries (those who traveled to spread the Gospel):**
Global Missionaries/Cross-Cultural Workers – These individuals travel to different parts of the world, often to remote or underserved areas, to share Christianity while helping meet local needs through education, healthcare, and community development.

16  **Lectors Officiants (those who read Scripture in worship services):**
Scripture Readers – In churches today, these individuals publicly read from the Bible during services, ensuring that scripture remains central in worship and teaching.

17  **Psaltists Officiants (those who led singing in worship):**
Worship Leaders – These leaders organize and lead congregational singing, guiding the church in musical worship through modern worship bands or choirs.

18  **Gravedigger Ministry (those who buried the dead):**
Funeral Ministry Teams – These volunteers help families navigate grief by organizing and supporting funeral services, providing care and comfort, and maintaining church cemeteries.

19  **Chaplains (those who ministered to prisoners):**
Prison/Hospital/Military Chaplains – They provide spiritual care and counseling to

people in specialized settings such as hospitals, prisons, or military bases, helping those in crisis connect with their faith.

20  **Armorers (those who provided for the physical needs of missionaries):**
    **Mission Support Teams** – These groups ensure missionaries and ministers are well-resourced, organizing funding, logistical support, and practical help to sustain those working in the field.

21  **Widows (those who dedicated themselves to prayer, service, and women's ministry):**
    **Women's Ministry Leaders** – These leaders focus on providing spiritual guidance, organizing prayer groups, and supporting other women through mentoring, Bible study, and community service.

22  **Deaconesses ministers (women who served in various capacities in the Church):**
    **Women's Ministry Directors** – They oversee ministries focused on women and children, organizing events, outreach, and discipleship activities that nurture faith and community engagement.

23  **Almoners (those who distributed alms to the poor):**
    **Benevolence Ministry Leaders** – These individuals oversee charitable funds and resources in the church, ensuring aid is distributed to those in financial need, both within the church and in the wider community.

24  **Baptism Officiants (such as deaconesses who baptized women):**
    **Baptism Coordinators** – Today, pastors or elders oversee baptism preparation and ceremonies, helping individuals understand the significance of baptism as part of their faith journey.

25  **Marriage Officiants:**
    **Wedding Officiants/Pastoral Counselors** – They officiate weddings, providing premarital counseling, guiding couples in biblical values, and ensuring Christian principles are upheld in marriage.

26  **Romance Pastoral Counseling:**
    **Marriage and Family Ministers including Romance Officiants** – They provide guidance on building healthy relationships, choosing a spouse, and maintaining a Christ-centered marriage, often working with couples before and after marriage.

# Conclusion

Volunteer ministers have always been and continue to be at the heart of the Church's mission. Through their selfless service, the Gospel has spread, and communities have been strengthened. *Ministry Sciences* seeks to explore and understand the historical, philosophical, and spiritual contributions of these ministers, offering a deeper appreciation for their role in building the Kingdom of God. Their work, rooted in faith and driven by a deep sense of calling, reflects the heart of the Gospel itself.

# Suggested Readings:

1. **"The Church of the Apostles"** by Everett Ferguson

    - This book explores the life, worship, and structure of the early Christian Church, with an emphasis on how the apostles and early believers built and led the church in the first centuries. It provides insights into the roles of volunteer ministers and the structure of the early church.

2. **"The Didache: The Teaching of the Twelve Apostles"**

    - An early Christian text, often referred to as a manual for church life in the first century. It gives practical instructions on the life of early Christians, including ministries like teaching, healing, and baptizing, and how they functioned in the early church.

3. **"Christianity Today's History of the Church"** (edited by Everett Ferguson)

    - This book provides a detailed look into the history of Christianity and the significant roles that volunteers, lay ministers, and part-time ministers played in building the early Church and shaping its mission and outreach.

4. **"The Apostolic Fathers"** by Michael W. Holmes

    - A collection of writings from the early church leaders known as the Apostolic Fathers. This book gives a firsthand account of how church leadership, including volunteer roles, developed in the first and second centuries.

5. **"The Complete Book of Everyday Christianity"** by Robert Banks and R. Paul Stevens

    - This book addresses how Christian faith can be integrated into every aspect of daily life, including part-time or volunteer ministry roles. It emphasizes that ministry isn't only for professional clergy but is the work of all believers.

6. **"Volunteer Church: Mobilizing Your Congregation for Growth and Effectiveness"** by Leith Anderson and Jill Fox

    - This modern text addresses the practical side of organizing and mobilizing volunteers in today's church. It offers tips on how to cultivate, train, and support part-time and volunteer leaders effectively.

7. **"The Master Plan of Evangelism"** by Robert E. Coleman

    - Focused on the methods of Jesus and the apostles, this book explores the simple yet effective ways early Christians spread the gospel, often through volunteer ministry. It provides a framework for modern-day evangelism based on these time-tested strategies.

8. **"The Early Church"** by Henry Chadwick

    - This classic work provides a comprehensive overview of the early Church, highlighting the role of volunteer ministers, laypeople, and women in ministry during the first centuries of Christianity. It helps readers see the roots of modern

volunteer ministry in the historical context.
9. **"Bi-Vocational: Returning to the Roots of Ministry"** by Mark A. Edington
   - This book examines the increasingly common role of bi-vocational ministers, who often work part-time or full-time in non-ministry jobs while also leading churches or ministries. It connects to the early church's example of leaders like Paul, who supported themselves through secular work while ministering.
10. **"The Shape of the Liturgy"** by Dom Gregory Dix
    - This in-depth exploration of Christian worship through the ages highlights the roles of various ministers, including lay volunteers, in the life of the Church. It provides insights into how these practices evolved and are adapted for modern ministry.

# Conclusion

## Concluding Chapter: Ministry Sciences—Empowering Every Christian to Serve

Christianity is at a pivotal moment in history, facing both incredible challenges and opportunities. With over 2.3 billion believers worldwide, the Church is a diverse and vibrant body of Christ, united in its mission but often divided in its approach. In the face of increasing cultural, social, and spiritual needs, a new understanding of ministry is emerging—one that recognizes the calling and gifting of every believer to serve in their unique way. *Ministry Sciences* is the key to unlocking this potential, creating a framework for effective, sustainable, and Spirit-filled ministry for all Christians, regardless of their role in the Church.

### Ministry Sciences: A Framework for Mobilizing the Church

*Ministry Sciences* combines biblical truths, theological insights, and practical methods to make ministry more effective, personal, and accessible. It acknowledges that ministry is not confined to professional clergy but extends to every believer who has been called and gifted by God to serve. The foundation of *Ministry Sciences* rests on the understanding that God's calling is woven into every believer's life and that ministry, in its many forms, is the natural outflow of the Christian experience.

### A Call to Rediscover Ministry in Every Life

Ministry is more than preaching from a pulpit or leading a congregation. It's the daily acts of love, service, and leadership that reflect Christ to the world. Whether through teaching, mentoring, counseling, caregiving, or simply offering a listening ear, *Ministry Sciences* invites all believers to explore how their unique gifts, talents, and experiences can be used for God's glory. This approach decentralizes ministry from the traditional pastor-centered model and empowers every believer to actively participate in the Great Commission.

In Romans 12:4-6, Paul reminds us of the diversity of gifts within the body of Christ: *"For just as each of us has one body with many members, and these members do not all have the same function, so in Christ we, though many, form one body, and each member belongs to all the others. We have different gifts, according to the grace given to each of us."* (Romans 12:4-6, NIV)

## Every Believer Called to Ministry

One of the greatest misunderstandings in Christian communities is the belief that only a select few are called to ministry. *Ministry Sciences* breaks down this false notion and reveals that **every believer is called to ministry**. Ephesians 4:11-12 emphasizes this truth by teaching that the role of church leaders is to equip the saints for the work of ministry: *"So Christ himself gave the apostles, the prophets, the evangelists, the pastors and teachers, to equip his people for works of service, so that the body of Christ may be built up."* (Ephesians 4:11-12, NIV)

Through *Ministry Sciences*, we explore the ways in which each person's calling and gifting can be understood, developed, and released into action. Whether through volunteer service, part-time ministry, or full-time vocational work, *Ministry Sciences* equips Christians to serve where God has placed them, in alignment with their specific calling.

## The Four Pillars of Ministry: Habits, Knowledge, Experience, and Commitment

At the heart of *Ministry Sciences* are four foundational pillars that represent the key elements of spiritual growth and effective ministry: **habits, knowledge, experience, and commitment**. These pillars offer a holistic approach to serving God and others.

1. **Habits**: Developing spiritual disciplines—like prayer, worship, and Bible study—is essential for drawing closer to God. These practices form the habits that sustain a believer's spiritual life and prepare them for ministry.
   *"Discipline yourself for the purpose of godliness."* (1 Timothy 4:7, NASB)

2. **Knowledge**: Gaining biblical and theological knowledge empowers believers to minister with wisdom and truth. Ministry Sciences emphasizes the need for every Christian to deepen their understanding of Scripture and apply it to their calling.
   *"All Scripture is God-breathed and is useful for teaching, rebuking, correcting and training in righteousness."* (2 Timothy 3:16, NIV)

3. **Experience**: Personal encounters with God, whether through worship, prayer, or the exercise of spiritual gifts, strengthen believers' faith and enrich their ability to serve. Ministry Sciences encourages Christians to embrace these transformative experiences as part of their ministry journey.
   *"They were all filled with the Holy Spirit and spoke the word of God boldly."* (Acts 4:31,

NIV)

4 **Commitment**: Ministry requires dedication, perseverance, and a willingness to sacrifice. Ministry Sciences equips believers to remain steadfast in their commitment to Christ, no matter the challenges they face.
*"Whoever wants to be my disciple must deny themselves and take up their cross daily and follow me."* (Luke 9:23, NIV)

## The Role of Christian Leaders Institute and Christian Leaders Alliance

Through organizations like *Christian Leaders Institute (CLI)* and *Christian Leaders Alliance (CLA)*, Ministry Sciences becomes a practical reality for those seeking to engage in ministry. These organizations offer free and low-cost ministry training, allowing believers to gain the knowledge, skills, and credentials necessary to serve without the financial burdens often associated with theological education.

Whether someone is called to be a volunteer minister, part-time servant, or full-time pastor, *CLI* and *CLA* provide pathways to help them explore their calling and step confidently into ministry. The accessibility of online courses, mentorship, and credentialing ensures that every believer can pursue their God-given purpose.

## A Call to Action: Discover Your Ministry

As we conclude this exploration of *Ministry Sciences*, the call is clear: **God has called and gifted every Christian to serve in ministry**. Whether you are a young believer, a seasoned leader, or someone simply searching for your place in God's plan, this is the moment to respond to that call. Ministry is not reserved for a select few; it is the responsibility—and the privilege—of every follower of Christ.

1 Peter 4:10 reminds us: *"Each of you should use whatever gift you have received to serve others, as faithful stewards of God's grace in its various forms."* (1 Peter 4:10, NIV)

**How is God calling you to serve?** Are you ready to explore your unique gifts and step into the ministry God has prepared for you?

This is your invitation to consider how you can serve in your family, your community, your church, and the world. Take a step today—whether through volunteering, mentoring, pursuing ministry training, or simply committing to intentional prayer and service. Through *Ministry Sciences*, you can discover the fullness of what God has called you to do.

## The Future of Ministry: A World Transformed

Imagine a world where every Christian is actively engaged in ministry, empowered by their gifts, and equipped to make a difference. Imagine churches filled with believers who are not just spectators but active participants in God's kingdom work. This is the future of ministry that *Ministry Sciences* envisions—a world where the body of Christ works in unity to advance the gospel, bring healing to the broken, and shine the light of Christ in every corner of society.

The time is now. God is calling. Are you ready to answer?

## Final Charge

As we conclude, let this be a charge to all who read these words: **Discover your ministry, step into your calling, and be a vessel of God's grace in the world**. Whether as a volunteer, a part-time servant, or a full-time minister, you have a role to play in the mission of God. *Ministry Sciences* equips you to serve faithfully, and God's Spirit will guide you every step of the way.

*"Go, therefore, and make disciples of all nations, baptizing them in the name of the Father and of the Son and of the Holy Spirit."* (Matthew 28:19, NIV)

The world is waiting, and God is calling—let us answer the call and transform the world through the love and power of Jesus Christ.

Made in the USA
Middletown, DE
06 November 2024